ESCAPE THE BLACK CLOUD OF HOUSEWORK

By

Laurel Zigler

ISBN: 1-4033-0354-1 (e-book)
ISBN: 1-4033-0355-X (Paperback)
ISBN: 1-4033-3464-1 (Hardcover)

This book is printed on acid free paper.

1stBooks - rev. 08/05/02

Prologue

As the clouds of my past fade away,
I uncover a bright new life of joy.
Anonymous

Preface

You know the feeling you get when you see flashing lights in your rearview mirror and hear sirens? That same feeling appears, every time you hear a siren. Naturally, your first response is to pull to the side of the road. All may go well, if there is plenty of room. What if the street is crowded with cars that are all stopped for a signal light? Do you get nervous or become rattled? In an effort to pull over you may end up crossways in the traffic, and you may even feel your self-esteem drop. You are sure the other drivers think you don't know how to drive.

Where did you get these feelings? Was it one incident or several that made you feel what you *always* feel at that moment? Could you change the way you feel? If so, how would you go about making those changes? We could call these siren feelings "Siren Fever."

We all get similar feelings from "The Black Cloud of Housework" when we get that phone call advising us that someone is dropping by the house in a few minutes. It may be a boss, a relative, or a friend. Everyone gets "a feeling," just as we get one when we hear a siren. The feeling may be one of panic, followed by a flurry of speed cleaning. It may be a dark feeling or a low self-esteem feeling, particularly if the visitor is a relative.

Some people live their lives with this cloud following them everywhere they go. Every day they endure the negative messages shooting at them from the cloud like bolts of lightning. These messages are the same for all housekeepers, from the most relaxed to the perfectionist. They say things such as: "You slob; you left laundry in the dryer." Or, "Who do you think you are? If people saw how you keep house they would know how you really are. They would know the real worthless you."

Often these clouds influence the lives of unknowing victims and even control part or all areas of their lives in some manner. I was surprised at the degrees of variation that I found in housekeepers who owned "Black Clouds."

One woman I interviewed, locked her family out of the house each day until she finished cleaning the house. When she let the children in the house for lunch, she made them eat cereal standing over the sink.

Another person put dirty dishes in the oven—and bathtub—until every dish in the house was dirty. When there were no more dishes, she stood for hours at the sink to wash them.

None of these people that I interviewed were aware of why they clean the way they do or where they got their housekeeping habits.

WHY DO PEOPLE CLEAN HOUSE THE WAY THEY DO?

Using a simple exercise when interviewing people about their individual housekeeping, I allowed them to go inside their hearts and heads to discover their basic beliefs. During this process, they were often able to pull information out of their subconscious to find out where they got their feelings and how they began. The information they discovered about themselves allowed them to disburse the cloud and bring sunlight and peace into their lives.

Some changed their housekeeping skills dramatically. Others made no housekeeping changes but cleaned with a different view, allowing them to let loose of the tether to the "Black Cloud." They were able to remove judgment and bring comfort and relaxation into their lives. The information learned from these interviews is the basis for this book.

This is a book, not only for learning about the feelings we have about housekeeping and how housekeeping relates to our lives. It is also a guide to making workable changes that will improve our lives.

I recommend that the readers complete the two exercises in the book before they begin to clean.

Acknowledgments

Writing this book has given me the opportunity to help others by sharing something I learned about myself.

I would like to thank the following people:

All the people who granted me interviews and shared all their housekeeping "Black Clouds" so that together we can find a way get light through those clouds. These people are the backbone of this book. My sister Dorsa, who during our visit to Phoenix, Arizona, helped me to see that I really could write a book; my high school classmate Judie Kleng, for writing her book and telling me that I should go for it, artist Bertha Metcalf and Gail Scott, and Ella Robinson, my copy editor.

Dedication

To my children and grandchildren.
You can accomplish anything
at any age.
I also dedicate this book to a
fifty-nine-year-old man who did not know
the toaster had a clean-out tray.

Contents

CHAPTER 1 <u>IN REALITY</u>

In reality… Cleaning house is part of life, as if raising children, working and paying taxes. Like it or not, housekeeping is in our lives. It is accepted by most and dreaded by all.

Why do some people clean and others do not? I heard once, "People who do not care about themselves do not clean house." I have not found this statement to be true. I have found that the commitment of house cleaning does not always reflect the success of a person's life at home or in a business. Although, housekeeping may often influence the way a person lives their individual life.

For example, I read in an Arizona newspaper that a woman left her home and did not tell any of her neighbors that she was going away. Noticing her disappearance, some of the neighbors decided to investigate. Approaching the house they encountered such a horrible stench that they called the police, fearing that she was dead inside.

When the police arrived, they did not find a body but were equally shocked at what they did find. The electricity to the house had been disconnected. Without air-conditioning, the house turned into an oven in the hot Arizona sun. The refrigerator contained huge webs of mold. Eight to twelve inches of walked down animal and human feces covered the bathroom floor. There was a narrow path throughout the house from room to room. The rest of the house contained piles of paper, cans, junk and rotting garbage, which according to the unopened mail found in the debris had been collecting for over five years.

The article stated that the woman had left her home and moved in with a co-worker, telling her friend that she was having some work done on her house and needed a place to stay.

A description of the woman by her co-workers and those who knew her was one of a person who was clean and well dressed. She had successfully held an executive position in a large company for years.

A city judge declared that her home was a health hazard to the neighborhood and sent city employees to clean up the mess. Donned in gas masks and armed with shovels, the workers filled many large roll-off garbage bins with the debris from the house. The woman paid a fine to cover the cost charged by the city for the clean up and was sentenced to take housekeeping classes.

This is probably one of the worse cases of refusal to clean house that I have ever heard. Still, she was successful in other areas of her life.

CHAPTER 2 WHY WE ARE THE WAY WE ARE

What makes us the type of housekeeper we are? What makes one person see housekeeping as a normal chore and others see it as a "Big Black Cloud" of doom hanging over their heads? Many people view it as a cloud with lightening bolts shooting out it, inflicting the pain of guilt, lost self-esteem and even feelings of failure. I believe our perception of housekeeping has a lot to do with the environment in which we lived as children. (Please refrain from jumping on the "Blame Our Parents Bandwagon.")

All of our beliefs and attitudes form, as we are children, growing up in our individual environments. I believe that housekeeping is a trait that also comes from our childhood.

Some mothers are obsessive about cleaning and demand that their children continually clean under a regimented rule. On the other hand, there are parents who seldom clean and raise their kids in disorganized or dirty environments. We may not follow in our parent's footsteps when it comes to cleaning house but living with that parent's housekeeping habits, helps us to design our own way of keeping house.

People who enjoy a clean house and put out the energy to clean cannot relate to someone who does not clean and visa versa. This inability to see the other's point of view often results in cliché relationships, which form only with others who have the same housekeeping lifestyle. Even with different choices about housekeeping many people, both the relaxed cleaner and the one who cleans too much, share feelings that they don't clean correctly or enough.

Often the attitudes we have about the way we keep house will project how we judge others and ourselves in all areas of our lives. I believe this is true because in our society, people often judge others by the way they keep house. The judging scale may look something like this: Immaculate, Lived In, Untidy, Dirty, Filthy or Garbage Dump.

I feel that each of us must look inside ourselves to understand why we have the beliefs and habits we live by. We also need to strive to understand and accept the beliefs and attitudes of others *without being judgmental*.

The first time I began to realize that people thought differently when it came to housecleaning-occurred while I was a young mother. It was traditional in our family for the women to clean the home of the new mother on the day that she and her baby were to come home from the hospital. This allowed her to care for herself and the baby, not having to do catch-up on housework that accumulated in her absence. (Husbands did little housework in those days and the mothers stayed in the hospital longer after the birth of a baby.)

3

The women in our family often chose to share our family housekeeping ritual with some of our closest friends by cleaning house for the new parents. The new mother usually appreciated a clean house. However, I remember one friend who did not seem so appreciative.

It was the time when a friend and her husband took their new infant out of town to visit relatives. She gave me the key to her house and asked me to feed the dog while they were away. Since I felt her house rated between "Lived In" and "Dirty," on the scale I mentioned earlier. I decided to use the family tradition as an excuse to clean her house. In all reality, I was so sure that once she saw how her home looked, all clean and shiny, she would fall in love with it and keep it that way forever.

When the couple returned a very pleased husband thanked me for the work I had done. My friend, however, with little enthusiasm simply said, "Thank you" And that was that. Within a month I was unable to tell that I had touched a thing *in her house.*

I had trouble in those days understanding how people could stand to sit in a house with any disarray. I was probably as immaculate as they came. At one point, a friend of mine told me that I even went too far because I emptied ashtrays while my company was still there and often after the ashtrays contained only a couple of cigarettes.

CHAPTER 3 <u>TO CHANGE</u>

I personally began to change my own cleaning habits after reading an article in Ann Landers' self-help column, and after seeing a special titled, *Life and Death,* on television.

The article was from a woman, who like her mother, was an immaculate housekeeper. When the daughter did not hear from her mother for several days, she decided to pay her a visit. The woman answered the door in her robe. She was not wearing make-up and her hair was uncombed. It was obvious that she was ill. When she saw her daughter, she began apologizing for the condition of the house, explaining that she was sick she had not vacuumed or dusted in days.

The house looked like a model home, as it always did. At that moment, the younger woman realized that she did not need to do a lot of her household duties on a daily basis. By vacuuming and dusting every other day and doing laundry twice a week, the daughter found a new freedom from her chores.

Often, we blindly follow our family traditions, which include the way we cook and clean house. We never question why we follow these rules; it is just some sort of unwritten rule that we obediently follow.

A story that comes to mind that best demonstrates this is the one of a woman fixing a meal for relatives at Christmas. As she prepared a ham, she cut about two inches off the end of the ham before cooking it. When her new sister-in-law asked her why she cut the ham in that fashion, she replied, "I don't know. My mother always did it that way." Days later she began thinking about it and called her mother. "Mom," she began, "why did you always cut two inches off the end of the ham when you cooked it?" Her mother replied, *"So it would fit in the pan."*

A television special titled, *Life and Death,* was the biggest event in my life in changing my outlook on cleaning house. The "life" part of the special was the day-by-day routine in the lives of a young couple from the moment they conceived a baby-following them through the ultrasounds, buying baby clothes, painting the nursery, Lamaze classes, and the delivery, to taking the baby home. It was beautiful and uplifting.

The "death" portion of the program was the philosophy of a lovely old man in a nursing home. He was in his eighties and had resided at the home for some time. The reporter questioned the gentleman about all aspects of his life, his profession, his family and his home. They showed pictures of an immaculate home in which he had resided for many years after the death of his spouse. He stated that he had always done all of his own housekeeping. His housekeeping skills were impressive. As the interview came to a close,

5

the reporter had one question for the old gentleman. "If you had your life to live over, what changes, if any, would you make?" Without hesitation, the old man replied, *"I would have cleaned house less and fed the pigeons in the park more."*

The program continued, showing the man having passed away in his sleep, the preparation of his body for burial and finally the funeral. As I watched the end of his life and the end of the program, I cried. I cried because a lovely person was making the transition from this world, where I was sure that he had touched so many lives in a positive way. I cried too, because he felt he had regrets, as small as they seemed. As I wiped away the tears, I vowed that I would not have the same regrets about housekeeping as the old gentleman. I would no longer allow chores to take time from me, robbing me of something that was more important to share in my life.

There were very definite, unwritten rules of society during the time I was raising my family. Because of these rules, I believed that being a good spouse and mother meant keeping an immaculate home and yard, having perfect children and attending church and PTA. However, as I looked back, I realized that it was already too late. I already shared regrets with the old gentleman. *I wish I had cleaned house less and played with my children more.*

I remember how I believed that I had to have a clean house, with laundry and dishes done, diapers folded, food prepared, lawn mowed, and the cars washed *before I could play.* Sadly, playing with my children was part of my schedule as my role of "Good Mother." However, what I remember most are the many times I planned to spend time with my children before they went to bed but ran out of time while doing chores.

Now, when I am around mothers with babies and little children, I always give this suggestion. "As tough as it seems at times, these are the good times, take time to enjoy them because one day you will wake up to discover that the children are twenty-six years old. It goes that fast." I say this to people I know and to strangers on the street. I only hope that they think about what I say, so they will not have too many regrets of time lost when their children become adults.

I know that by now, you are wondering when will this woman get around to talking about cleaning the house? We will get there soon enough.

Before we begin, I suggest that you take some time to look within yourself to see why you have the cleaning habits you posses. Once you have that understanding, the cleaning part may be much easier. You may even be able to rid yourself of old beliefs and rules, allowing you more freedom in your life. You may have more freedom because you clean less or more freedom because you free yourself from negative feelings for the way that you chose to clean house. To help you understand, let me share with you what some individuals have found out about themselves and about the way they keep house.

CHAPTER 4 NICK AND MARIA

One couple with whom I spoke was in the process of building a business of their own. Nick and Maria went to their jobs during the day and worked on their business in the evenings and on weekends. It left them little time to spend with their two small children.

After some time, they had built their business to the point where Maria was able to quit her job and stay home, working exclusively on their business and spending time with the children. Maria felt their plan was very successful. Nick, on the other hand began to display disapproval about the way Maria cleaned the house.

When it became apparent that they were arguing more and more about housework, they decided to sit down and design a plan that satisfied both of them. Nick felt that Maria should keep a cleaner house now that she was home all the time. Maria pointed out that he needed to realize that the time she spent on their business was to be considered the same time that she had spent on her previous job. It was time allotted for her to work on the business, not to do housekeeping. Although Maria did not spend a full eight hours on the business, she spent the remainder of the time with the children. Maria also reminded Nick that she still spent the same amount of time on the business in the evenings and on weekends that she always had. She felt that he was asking too much of her.

Accepting that Maria may be correct. Nick decided that he would be more responsible in sharing the housework. He promised to stop dropping his clothes where he took them off and he would iron his work shirts. He would also take turns doing the dishes and laundry and be sure the kids cleared the table after meals.

Even with Nick's help, Maria found it difficult to clean house to his expectations. When she felt the house was becoming unbearable for Nick. She would put work on their business aside and thoroughly clean the house for several days. She would then work on the business for several days to catch up, ignoring the house. Without doing maintenance cleaning on a daily basis the cleaning never lasted.

One day over coffee with a friend, Maria was expressing her concerns about her inability to keep the house as Nick thought she *should*. Her friend suggested that Maria take the word *should* out of her vocabulary, indicating that the word produce feelings of *wrongdoing* or guilt for *not doing*. The friend reminded Maria that she was *never wrong in any choice she made about how she cleaned her house.*

Later, Maria thought about what her friend had said. It was true. When she cleaned house, she felt as she was doing it because Nick expected and wanted her to, not because of what she wanted. Perhaps the word *should* did have a lot of power.

Later that evening, Maria told Nick what her friend had shared with her and requested that he refrain from using the word *should* in his discussions with her about housecleaning. Nick became angry, accusing her of trying to find an excuse for not doing the housework. After he cooled down, Nick apologized and promised he would change the way he made suggestions or requests of Maria. He also agreed to let her tackle her share of the housekeeping on her own schedule.

Once Nick no longer made negative comments about Maria's housekeeping, Maria stopped feeling that she was wrong or bad when she did not clean. She found it easier to do the housework. She discovered that cleaning in small intervals, when needing a break from work, was a perfect balance for her. She was able to do both jobs efficiently enough, that their business grew and the house was easier to keep clean.

Delighted with the housekeeping chores and the business Maria accomplished, Nick began designing and organizing easier methods for doing work in their business and their home. These new methods made both jobs easier for all the family members.

As humans, we object to being told what to do. We tolerate it from the government and from our employers but much like a child in toilet training, when it is something in an area of our life we can control, we may rebel. If we can discuss our feelings, we then have a chance of changing them. We gain insight within ourselves or see that the changing of words in our conversations may be all it takes to make workability come to those areas of our lives.

CHAPTER 5 <u>EVA</u>

Eva told me that she felt guilty because she was a very bad housekeeper. I asked her to tell me all she could about the way she kept her house and why she felt she judged herself that *type of housekeeper.* I asked her to talk until I told her to stop and if necessary, to repeat herself, just as long as she continued talking.

I listened, sitting motionless and keeping constant eye contact. After talking for about twenty minutes, Eva paused, and then she said, "That is all there is and now I know what I have to do." Here is her story.

She began by telling me about how guilty she felt by not providing a clean home for her teenage son. Even worse, she did not even have a couch on which he could sit. Eva went on to tell me that she had built the house in which she and her son now lived but being a single mother, she had run out of funds before completion. Her parents moved from another town to help her finish the home she was building. However, the first thing they did was to build on an addition in which they were to live.

Instead of installing the solar heating unit that Eva had already purchased, her parents chose to install floor heaters. To conceal the heaters, they had to pour new concrete over the existing floors. At the time of our interview the solar heat still had not been installed and the concrete floors were still uncovered. When the workers poured the additional concrete, they never raised the original drain in the floor in the family room. Using a stick, they cleared the concrete from around the drain, forming a cup in the floor in which Eva's son and his friends later used to putt golf balls.

Later work on Eva's section of the house still never resulted in completion of her home. Since her parents disapproved of the way she kept house, Eva felt that was the reason the work stopped.

Eva was a lover of animals and often felt closer to animals than people. To demonstrate this and how different of a housekeeper she was, she shared with me that one of her dogs had delivered and raised a litter of puppies in the center of the living room. Eva assured me that the house never smelled because she swept up the puppy droppings, once they dried.

At the time of our conversation Eva had six dogs, which had the run of the house and were often in the house all day. She would put them out when she went to work but when their barking disturbed her parents; they would put the dogs back in the house. Eva repeatedly asked her parents to leave the dogs outside during the day but they refused. Locked in the house all day with nothing to do, the dogs destroyed her furniture, completely dismantling the couch. Unable to justify purchasing another couch for the dogs to destroy did not alleviate the guilt Eva felt by not having a couch for her son or his friends.

Eva's son had a baseball card collection that numbered in the thousands. He kept them in stacks piled around the house. The dogs often chewed and urinated on the baseball cards. I could tell that this really upset Eva and added greatly to her guilt about the way she kept house.

Continuing her discussion, Eva stated that she had always been *that type of housekeeper*. The only time she kept a clean house was for two years when she was first married. That was the time in her life when she was the *happiest* she had ever been.

Although Eva was an attractive woman and dressed nicely, she said that she was unable to keep a male relationship in her life. Once her dates saw her house, they ran as fast as they could right out of her life.

Several weeks before our meeting, a friend had offered to help her clean her home. The two of them had spent several days cleaning her house and when they finished, Eva admitted *it looked pretty good*. She now had a preview of how her house could look with some efforts from herself and her son.

It appeared that Eva believed that she only cleaned when she had a man in her life and was happy. Since her parents had the money to finish the building on her home, they gained control over part of her life. The only control she seemed to have against them was her refusal to comply with their housekeeping rules. It appeared that Eva even used her housekeeping as a way to protect herself from the very relationship that she thought she wanted with a member of the opposite sex.

I was bursting with excitement at the discoveries that Eva was making but I remained quiet. (For me, that is a challenge.) As Eva continued to talk, she began to see solutions.

Eva realized that she had all the ingredients for a happy life with her son and parents. She did not need a man in her life to be happy. She saw that a storage system would protect her son's baseball card collection. Her goal was to get his help in sorting and filing the cards, then enroll him in helping her clean the house. Together they could design the type of home they both wanted, *a clean, happy home*.

Unable to see her life without her pets, Eva admitted that she knew they needed training. She decided that she was going to have to keep the dogs out of the house when she was not home to discipline them. Eva was going to have a serious talk with her parents about her wishes to keep the dogs outside during the day. If that failed, she would have to put locks on her doors to which her parents had no keys. By confronting her parents, Eva could be dealing with some issues that she had never approached before, some relating as far back as her childhood. However, she felt that standing

11

up to her parents would demand respect from them and could possibly open new avenues in their relationship.

It was a big step for Eva to face her fear about relationships. Once she had a clean house, she realized that she would be taking a risk to have a relationship with a man. It would leave her wide open for rejection if a man chose not to stay in her life. She would then have to accept that it was not the house that caused him to go away.

It was exciting for me to see her face light up as she started finding solutions to solving problems that related, not only to housekeeping but other areas of her life. I wish I could take some credit for releasing Eva from the "Black Cloud" of housekeeping that shadowed her life but I cannot. It was listening to her own conversation and responding to those conversations, then finding solutions, which gave her inspiration.

No one really cared if Eva cleaned her home, with maybe the exception of her son but he was not doing the housework either. Any attempt by others to get Eva to clean her house was a *control problem*, owned by that person.

As much as Eva told herself that she was a bad mother and a slob of a person, nothing I saw substantiated any of those feelings. She was attractive, well dressed and well educated. She had just designed a dog food and her dog food business was off to an explosive beginning.

Instead of looking far ahead into the future, to when Eva would finally have a clean house with nice furniture, she began looking at what she would get now *while she cleaned*. This allowed her to remove the dread and destroy the vision of a house buried in tons of work. Her ability to get the immediate satisfaction of protecting her son's baseball cards from the animals would help alleviate some of her housekeeping guilt.

Eva could see that training the dogs would allow her to buy a couch. By cleaning a section of the room for the new couch, she could enjoy both the couch and the dogs. She could then continue cleaning her home, step by step, day by day. Most of all, Eva saw the possibility of creating a bond with her son as they worked together in building the type of home in which they could both be happy to live.

I hope that sharing with you what other people found within themselves in the area of housekeeping might show you that as humans; feelings control all our actions in all areas of our lives. If you want to know why you behave the way you do in any area of your life, you need to closely examine your feelings to get to the reasons for your actions. The design of the following pages will help you discover what makes you the type of housekeeper you are and why.

Do the Exercise

CHAPTER 6 THE EXERCISE

If you decide to skip any pages in this book, please be sure that you do not miss the following pages. This procedure will allow you to look inside your heart and your head at your most inner-self. You may discover something about yourself that you never knew existed. Most people are surprised or shocked at what they find out about themselves, when they do this simple exercise. Are you ready to begin?

You must do this exercise when you are able to relax and think clearly. Preferably you will either be alone or in a quiet place with a friend or family member, who is willing to be only a listener. Your listener will not speak or offer any suggestions or respond in any way to the things you say. Their role is to be that of a sounding board. This person must agree to sit perfectly still. They must keep constant eye contact, *showing no response* to anything you say. That means that they cannot smile or even raise an eyebrow. Their gaze is to keep you focused and on track. Their undivided attention will encourage you to keep talking until the time has ended. You are to talk to your sounding board for no less than twenty minutes. You will begin by saying anything you wish, as long as it pertains to the way you keep house. You may feel at times that you are getting off the subject but go with the flow and see where it leads you. If you are positive that you have left the subject, return as quickly as possible to your feelings about housekeeping.

Some of you may feel that you may not have anyone that you would like to have as your sounding board. Perhaps you feel this exercise is too personal to share with anyone else. If you are one of these people, then you will take quiet time by yourself for the exercise.

- Find a quiet, secluded spot.
- Take several pencils or pens, a tape recorder, or a friend with you.
- If alone, write as fast and as hard as you can. Write the first things that come to mind, no matter how stupid you think they sound. Start with the statement: "I feel I am a_____housekeeper." And continue with, "I feel I am that type of housekeeper because_____." Write for no less than twenty minutes without stopping. Repeat yourself if necessary. Just keep writing.

If using a tape recorder or a human sounding board, talk continually for twenty minutes, beginning with one of the previous statements. (Use a focal point when using a tape recorder.) Repeat yourself if necessary, but you must KEEP TALKING.

I have listed some questions that you can read BEFORE you begin the session. Do not refer to these questions during this exercise. It may break your train of thought.

You may feel as if you are rambling and you may even feel embarrassment if you are talking to a real person. These are feelings that you must overcome. Brainstorming in voice or on paper will allow you to discover things you never knew existed.

BELOW ARE SOME QUESTIONS THAT YOU CAN ASK YOURSELF, BEFORE THE EXERCISE.

- What type of housekeeper am I? By what standards?
- Where did I get these standards?
- Do I care what others think or say about my housekeeping? If so, why?
- What do *I think* others say about my housekeeping? How does this make me feel?
- If asked, how would I describe the way I keep house?
- How do I feel about myself because of the way I clean house?
- Do I feel my house is too dirty or too clean?
- Do I feel guilt associated with the way I keep house? If so, why?
- How would I feel in my life, if my house were exactly the way I would like it to be? Would my home be cleaner or more relaxed?
- How would I feel living in such a home?
- How would I feel if I had time to spend with my family or doing things I wanted to do and have a clean home?
- How would I feel if there was no dread or guilt in my life concerning my housekeeping?
- If someone came in and cleaned my house for me one time, what would I be willing to do to keep it that way?
- How much time would I be willing to spend on housekeeping each day?

QUESTIONS TO ASK YOURSELF AFTER THE EXERCISE

(Write down the answers.)

- What kind of things did you find out about yourself?
- Were you surprised to find out exactly how you do feel?
- Did you discover the reasons you clean house the way you do?
- Did you find out where your standards came from and why you adopted them as yours?
- Did you discover that the way you clean house relates to someone else or the way *someone else thinks you should keep house?*
- Did you find you had feelings of being a bad housekeeper because you *cleaned too much,* according to someone else's standards?
- Did you learn that no matter how hard you tried, you believed that you could never become a good enough housekeeper? Did you believe that you could never clean as well as Mom, Sis, or someone else who has influence over you?
- Did you see that you were obsessive in your cleaning and exhausted yourself every day trying to keep a model home, spotless for any visitor any time of the day?
- Did you find that you feel less of a person because of the way you *think* society views the way you clean your house?
- Did you discover that your housekeeping keeps people away because they feel uncomfortable in such a sterile atmosphere? Or in such a relaxed atmosphere?
- Did you learn that *you are the person* that bestows on yourself feelings of inadequacy concerning your housekeeping?
- Were there words like, slob, bad person, perfectionist, obsessive housekeeper or other names that came up in your conversation in which *you used to describe yourself?*

What inner feelings did you notice? (Sadness, anger, worthlessness, picked on, fatigue.)

CHAPTER 7 DISCOVER YOUR FEELINGS ABOUT HOUSEWORK

(ARE THEY NEGATIVE OR POSITIVE?)

When you think people are coming to visit on a moment notice? Is it a positive or negative feeling? Example: JENNY CALLED; SHE IS ON HER WAY OVER. What does your self-talk say to you? Does it go something like this?

- Jenny is coming to *visit me*, not to do a housekeeping inspection.
- Oh no, there is laundry in the dryer that needs folding and the baby has toys on the living room floor.
- Well, here comes Jenny. She knows that the house is a mess. It always is what else is new? She knows *I am a slob.*
- Jenny keeps a neater house than I do but she is not the type of person who places a lot of stock in how others keep house. If she were, she would not come to visit me.
- Jenny likes me for myself. It does not matter to her if I am a more relaxed housekeeper.
- Jenny and I are friends. We share a lot of likes and dislikes. We usually agree on all aspects of child rearing but she keeps a neater house. I am on the other hand, very good with finances. We are able to buy more and do more than Jenny and her husband.
- Oh good, Jenny is coming. The house is a mess but I am going to run to the donut shop and get those donuts she loves to have with our coffee.
- I am so glad Jenny is coming. I miss her. We need to make more time to get together more often.
- It has been so long since Jenny last visited. Wait until she sees how much the baby has grown. Now where are those baby pictures? Maybe I will find them on the kitchen table when I clear a spot for us to sit and have tea.
- I love to have Jenny come and visit me. We are such good friends. Jenny knows she is welcome anytime by just stopping by the house. We never set a date unless we plan to go out for entertainment.

- If you have negative feelings about a person coming to visit, you need to examine that relationship, especially if your self-talk goes something like this:
- Oh no, Jenny is coming. The last time she was here, she said the house smelled. What will she find to complain about today?
- The last time I went to see Jenny, she asked that I keep my baby on a blanket so he could not spit up or wet on the carpet. I was exhausted by the time I left. Nine-month-old babies are hard to keep in one place. It would have been easier if she would let me use her playpen. Jenny said that it was unsanitary to put my baby in her babies' playpen.
- Oh great... Jenny is coming. Last time she had just come from the beauty shop and she had the nerve to tell me that it looked as if I needed to make an appointment myself. When she left, she *accidentally* left a business card for her beautician and a card for a local cleaning agency.

Housekeeping disputes are dealt with and handled by the family members who live in the home. Any challenge from friends or family members outside the home seldom involves housekeeping. It is usually about a control problem or it involves some other issue. LOOK CLOSELY AT ANY SOURCE FROM WHICH YOU RECEIVE NEGATIVE FEELINGS ABOUT HOUSEKEEPING, OR ANYTHING ELSE.

When you did **The Exercise**, you had a chance to see any negative feelings you had about your housekeeping. Most of them may have been a surprise to you. Some you knew very well. Your job is to rid yourself of these negative feelings. Do you see that the way you clean house is up to you and it is your decision to do it your way? *It is no one else's business how you clean your house.* You have permission from the "Broom God" to be in total control *of your home.*

CHAPTER 8 SHARING THE WORK

If you live with others, you must work out a plan that works for all. If each of you give and take, you will arrive at rules that will make everyone happy. It will not work if you decide that you never want to touch a window or a toilet again as long as you live. Other members of the household may feel the same but everyone has to take their turn. That is how it works.

In a family, the mom is not the servant. Chores are for everyone. Children need to learn how to take care of themselves. Children also need to know how it is in the real world when it comes to household duties. Both parents need to help with chores and the training of the children.

Some parents give allowances for chores children do around the house. I feel that there is nothing wrong with allowances. An allowance gives a child the chance to handle money and to learn from it. However, I feel that children should get allowances as *their share of the family income.*

We want our school-age children to attend school. Therefore, school is considered to be *their job.* Children who are not yet school age will receive an allowance when the parents want to start teaching the child about handling money. In the meantime, the toddler learns to be part of the family unit without pay. It is the duty of all active family members to help with household chores. It is fine for your child to earn money to cut the neighbor's lawn but cutting his own lawn is considered part of his chores. Everyone in the family, who is old enough to run the mower, should receive training in cutting the lawn.

Often household residents select chores for which they want responsibility. Family members will select duties *peacefully and fairly* or the parents will assign chores. Chore assignments that are carved in stone will not allow for flexibility. Sons need to learn how to do dishes, the laundry, iron and mend. Daughters need to know how to mow a lawn. They also need to know how to wash a car, change the oil in a car and to fix a flat tire. Most of all, everyone needs to be flexible enough to take out the garbage or do a load of laundry if the person scheduled for that task is not home.

There is no reason for arguing over tasks handled by family members. Fighting usually alerts a parent that someone is avoiding his or her chores. Here is where allowances can be cut. Be clear that allowances are not strictly for chores completed but for being an active family member. Inactive family members do not deserve allowances. Just as inactive employees do not get salaries.

As a perfectionist, it was very difficult for me to live with the way my children did certain household jobs. I often felt it was easier to just do a job myself, than to do it again after a child tried their hand at it. This made it easy for me to restrict my children in the areas in which they helped with chores. What I did not realize was that I was limiting their learning and doing too much for them.

You must refrain from redoing any job your child has finished. Practice makes perfect or better, anyway. Doing a job again, after a child does it, sends a message to them that they are unable to do it correctly. If you continue to redo a job after a child, soon the child will stop trying.

Think about it. How would you feel if it seemed that you could never do anything right? Perhaps someone already did that to you in the past or possibly it is being done to you in the present.

Monitoring the job while your child is working will assist your child in completing their task. It teaches them to follow through until the job is finished. Make gentle reminders. Point out things that would make the room nicer. For example: "I think that Teddy would look so much nicer if he was sitting up on his shelf instead of lying down. Let's try it and see." When the child sets Teddy up, say: "Yes, that is better. Now people can see his beautiful eyes and nice smile." Asking a child if they can see anything else that needs to be done will produce instant blindness in your child. Don't do it

I suggest that you do a form of inspection. (Don't think army.) Inspection is when you view the job once it has been completed. Compliment what the child has done. THAT'S ALL.

Do not point out imperfections. If you feel that the child could use some suggestions, save it until the *next time* the child is doing the same job. Approach it by offering a suggestion during the monitoring time. You can handle it something like this.

"Sarah, you are doing a wonderful job. When I was little, I think one of the hardest jobs in cleaning my room was getting the bedding straight on the bed. Let me show you how my mother taught me to get them straight." After demonstrating how to line up the sheets, blankets and the spread, you have *helped her make her bed*. This will make her very happy and now she knows how to line up the bedding so it hangs evenly. From that day on, compliment her on how much better her bed looks; each time she does it nicer than the time before. (Ignore the times it looks awful.) If your daughter asks for additional instruction on how to make her bed and to get the blankets straight, be careful. Let me tell you why.

My son was about five years old. He told me that he was having trouble getting his bedding straight on his bed and asked if I would show him how to do it again. At first, I stood in the doorway and advised him what to do. He just could not seem to get it even. It was like cutting off table legs to get the table even. He would pull up one end and it would be too high, then he would pull down the other end and it was too low. Even when I tried to help him, he kept getting the blankets or spread uneven. Finally losing my patience, I grabbed the bedding. "First you do this, then you do that, then you do this." I made his bed giving full step-by-step instructions as I went along. When I finished, I looked up at a smug, smiling five-year old who had just tricked his mother into making his bed for him.

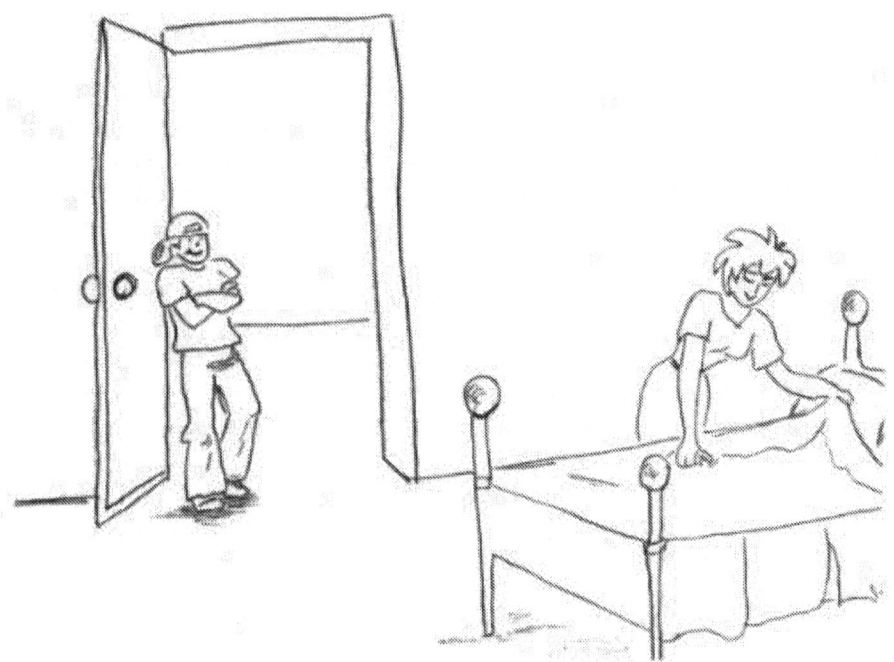

I remember clearly the day I discovered another message I was sending my children by limiting their chores to certain areas of housekeeping. It was a rainy day. The humidity was high. I was sweating over an ironing board, while my daughters, ages twelve and fourteen were laying on the carpet in front of the television. The task seemed endless and my anger began to escalate. The self-talk began. First I was complaining to myself about how much ironing there was, and then it turned to something about being nothing but a slave. As I paused to take a drink of ice water, I thought. *"What is wrong with this picture?"* I am ironing my daughter's clothes and they are watching television.

When they were smaller, they begged to iron and I would let them iron flat pieces, such as pillowcases or some of their dad's handkerchiefs. I never ironed them myself but they were good for the children to practice on. I believed that ironing to them was nothing but playing at being a mom. After all, I did not want them running around in wrinkles because they ironed their own clothes. What would people think when they saw my children in anything but perfectly ironed clothes? It never entered my mind that they may think the children ironed their own clothes.

I interrupted their television with an announcement that we were all going to the laundry room for a lesson on sorting clothes and running the washer and dryer. I received a raised eyebrow or two and some suspicious looks. After the clothes-washing lesson, we returned to the ironing board for an ironing lesson. Following the ironing lesson, one daughter politely asked, "Why do we have to do *your job?*" It was not my daughter's fault that they thought ironing was my job, it was my perfectionism that laid out the rules, written or unwritten.

I am not saying that ended my laundry and ironing days. It did not. Kids are very smart and as parents, we have to do all we can to keep ahead or at least keep up with them.

The girls and I took turns doing the laundry. We each had certain scheduled days for laundry duty, which lasted two or three days at a time. It took a surprisingly short time before I discovered that when one daughter did the laundry, the folded clothes placed on my bed for me to put away, harbored no white clothing. The stacks contained only colors of pale blues and pinks. No amount of instruction seemed to allow my husband, our preschool son or myself to wear white underwear. My daughter would look at me like she understood my recap of separating colors then again deliver pastel laundry to my room. It was obvious that new rules had to be designed.

Under the new rules, each daughter would now be entirely responsible for her own clothes. The girls' duties no longer included doing laundry for their parents or for their little brother. That would be my responsibility.

You have no idea how liberated I felt when I would hear one of them say, "Oh, I almost forgot; I have to wash my gym clothes for tomorrow." Do you know how surprised I was, when they seldom left for school in clothes that looked like they slept in them? However, if their clothes were not up to my perfect standards, I practiced looking the other way. It was a big lesson for the girls and a HARD one for me. My daughters became adults and my grandchildren go to school looking presentable.

It is important for family members to realize that they all have to pitch in and help if mom is going to bring in a second income. No mother wants to nag her family to get help with the housework. Often mothers are viewed as housekeeper/slaves, like my daughters thought it was MY JOB. A family is, in real life, a group of *roommates*. We all need to share the chores.

Sharing chores sounds good to Mom but if she isn't careful, she may still find herself nagging to get help with the chores or she may easily slip back into doing it herself. *We must not do this.* When a chore needs done, do not argue; do not ask. Simply tell the family member that the garbage needs taken out *now.* You will get a dirty look as they grudgingly head for the kitchen. Most of us will react to such behavior by telling that person, "Forget it." *Then we go and do it ourselves.* Keep in mind that you do not need to have helpmates that jump up with a smile to take out the garbage. Do you smile when it is your turn to take out the garbage?

Children learn that they are valuable cogs in the machinery called OUR HOME. They are proud that their presence helps the home run more smoothly and that they feel needed.

I believe that children need to learn how to clean and to clean properly. I feel that the best rule for any home is IF YOU GET IT OUT, PICK IT UP. Also: IF IT IS YOURS, PUT IT AWAY. On the other side of the coin, once we have trained our children to clean house, we can allow our older children to be in charge of their own rooms. (As long as they do not violate safety or health codes.) For mothers who shudder at this thought, keep the child's door closed and avoid going in whenever possible.

Everyone wins if you let your family roommates be in charge of the chores they like the best. My girls loved to cook and since I didn't, that worked out quite well. This is not counting the time my youngest daughter put the remainder of the cookie dough down the sink and my father had to come over with his plumbing snake and open the drain. When children cook, accept that when they clean up, they often use a dishcloth filled with wet flour to wipe down the counters and the front of the cupboards.

In spite of the clogged drains and the floured cupboards, I have fond memories of those meals provided by my children. Even though I am sure I have eaten hundreds, to this day, I get a craving for PIZZA PINWHEELS that my daughter's Dee and Lindy made. I am still unable to eat stew without remembering the great BOY SCOUT STEW made by my son Dion.

CHAPTER 9 DARE TO BE DIFFERENT

Doing things differently-will not make *you wrong*. Some people can bowl or play a good game of golf or tennis but are unable to play the violin. On the other hand, a great violinist may be unable to play a decent game of any kind. Is one or the other considered to be a better person? Both are experts in their field. Do you see that you are able to be a great mother, raise good children and be less than a perfect housekeeper? Can you be a great citizen and make differences in others lives, yet seem to be unable to communicate with your own family members in the way you wish you could. Perhaps you are able to climb Mt. Everest using all the necessary hiking gear, but when it comes to putting up a curtain rod you are the first to call a handyman. We all possess different talents, likes and dislikes. It is no one's business what choices other people make in his or her lives.

My best friend Janice and I were a very good example of how people are different. Janice and I had our first and second daughters born within two months of each other. It was as if we had two sets of twins between us. Like all mothers we loved dressing up our little girls and showing them off. Since we spent so much time together, shopping was also something we shared. Naturally the baby section of every store was our main target. Janice headed for the shoe department and I went directly to the bonnet displays. I loved baby hats. Shoes never attracted much of my attention. My babies' feet were so chubby that it was difficult to find shoes to fit them. They usually wore the famous TV booties made of corduroy.

Janice's babies had tiny feet and could wear any shoe in the store but her babies usually had very little hair. It always amazed me that because her babies lacked hair, she showed so little interested in bonnets.

We were quite a pair walking down the street with our stroller's side by side. My babies, who had plenty of hair, wore bonnets and were shoeless. Janice had babies that were bald-headed and wore fancy shoes.

Which mother was the better mother? Which mother was right? Do you see what I am trying to get you to see? Everything about you is your decision. Other peoples' views or opinions *about you and what you do,* is really NONE OF YOUR BUSINESS. *Get over worrying about what other people think*. Do in your life what makes you happy, as long as it is moral and legal and causes no one else pain.

CHAPTER 10 IT IS YOUR DECISION

I am willing to bet that you arrived at one of two decisions after doing **The Exercise**.

1. You decided that you like the way you keep house and you plan to continue doing it the same way. However, you may now feel better doing it *your way* because you can see yourself doing it *guilt* free. If this is your decision, I ask you to still read the rest of the book. There may be some suggestions that will help you.

2. You may have discovered what held you back or what pushed you. Perhaps you feel released somehow and you can make changes that will be beneficial to you. Possibly an understanding of yourself may allow you to change the way you clean house. You may have decided to do more housecleaning or you may have decided to do less cleaning.

The following pages will tell you how to reach your own goals at your own pace. You will learn how to organize without becoming a clean freak so that your housekeeping *works for you* in your family and in your life.

REREAD EACH SECTION BEFORE YOU START

By reading each section BEFORE you begin cleaning, you will know what direction you will be taking and what tools you need for the most efficient cleaning day.

CHAPTER 11 BEGIN CLEANING (FRONT ROOM)

LIST OF ITEMS YOU MAY NEED:
Soap, sponges, bucket of very warm water
Window cleaner, or vinegar and water
Upholstery cleaner
Plastic drop cloths
Wood soap
Lemon oil furniture polish to treat the wood
Furniture polish of your choice
Sponge mop (optional)
String mop
Floor wax, wood or vinyl
Grout cleaner
Carpet cleaner
Tub and tile cleaner
Bleach
Cardboard boxes, large
Small containers or boxes, one for each large cardboard box

LIST OF ITEMS YOU WILL NEED IF YOU DECIDE TO PAINT:
White paint (flat)
Water-base semi-gloss wall paint (off white, beige tones or color of your choice)
Enamel semi-gloss paint to match wall paint
Enamel semi-gloss paint for toe-space in kitchen (black)
Paint thinner
Paint brushes
Paint roller and roller pan
Masking tape
Ladder or step stool
Additional plastic drop cloths
Paint handle extension
Plenty of rags

Front room
"Obtain SIX large cardboard boxes and SIX smaller boxes in which to place tiny items." Label each large box as follows and place a smaller box in each of the large boxes:
      1. FRONT ROOM
      2. GARBAGE

3. GIVE AWAY (for friends or family)
4. DONATE
5. STORAGE
6. NOT FOR THIS ROOM

Place a chair in the middle of the living room, facing one wall of your choice. Sit down, lean back and look at the wall. Is there a window? Is there a door? Are there any built in bookcases or shelves? Look at the furniture against the wall, items hanging on the wall and anything four to six feet from the wall. (Anything in this space belongs to that wall.)

How many pieces of furniture are there? Are there window coverings, drapes, curtains, mini-blinds or verticals? Are there boxes or stacks of things, plants or items that catch dust?

First, move everything away from the wall. Move it past the six-foot line, out into the center of the room. (Do not block your access to the wall) Place any items that you will not return to that wall area into the correct cardboard box. The box labeled, FRONT ROOM will hold items that you may or may not use later in the room. Place very small items, such as marbles, paper clips, pens, coins, hair barrettes, etc., in the smaller box or container for each labeled box.

Take everything off the windows, built-ins and walls, including electrical receptacle covers. Place covers to soak in warm, soapy water and put the screws to soak in a small container, such as a jar or drinking glass for safekeeping. Screws will slip down a drain before you realize they are missing. You now have a naked wall and six feet of cleared floor space.

If the ceiling surface is smooth, you will want to wash it. Use a ladder or step stool to reach the ceiling safely. I personally find a good sponge mop ideal for washing the ceiling. However, you will need to get on a ladder or step stool to wash next to the walls and in the corners by hand. Don't worry about getting water on the wall or the floor, unless the floor has carpet. If your floor has carpeting, cover the carpet with a plastic drop cloth. Please do be careful that water *does not get into the open electrical receptacles*. The only way to clean a ceiling that is porous or acoustical is to paint.

Wash the wall, including the window, door, shelves, etc. Using whatever cleaning method and equipment you desire.

Examine the clean ceiling and wall. Do they need repair or paint? If so, now is the time to do both. After completing repairs, begin by painting the ceiling. Use a flat white paint. I have found that the cheaper "ceiling" paints are often thin and do not cover as well. I end up using more paint in the long run, not to mention having to paint the ceiling several times. Regular flat paint is, in my opinion, the best way to go. If the ceiling is flat, a roller designed for the flat surfaces will work very well. Otherwise, use a fluffy roller or scored sponge roller, designed for easy coverage for porous surfaces.

Paint along the wall and corners with a brush, painting down on the wall a couple of inches. Do this only if you are painting the walls too, even if they are to be a different color. If you are not painting the walls at this time, then neatly join the paint to the wall. (Be careful not to have runs in the paint on the overlap on the wall.) You will be able to paint the remainder of the ceiling with a paint roller. Use a paint handle extension. Extension handles are very inexpensive at the paint store. You can also use a broom or rake handle that screws or slips into the paint roller handle.

Paint the wall after-covering window facings, any wood trim, doors, shelves, etc., with masking tape. It is best to paint these areas with enamel paint. It is harder to clean up your painting tools when using enamel but the paint wears better and is easier to keep clean.

If you plan to paint the wall later, replace all electrical plug-in and light switch covers, until you are ready to paint. (It takes less time to remove them, than to mask them with tape.)

If you feel that you may be painting another section of ceiling and wall today, place the roller and brushes in a bucket of water. Tightly close the lid on the paint can. Put enamel tools in a container of paint thinner. If you are not going to do any more painting today, *clean your paint equipment now*.

WARNING: Never have opened PAINT THINNER in the same room as a GAS WATER HEATER or near any GAS APPLIANCE THAT HAS AN OPEN FLAME. **A FLASH FIRE MAY OCCUR.**

Clean the floor. If it is a vinyl floor covering, clean thoroughly with a mop or scrub brush and plenty of soapy water. If there is wax build up, use a floor stripper to remove the old wax. Wax with a clear acrylic floor wax. If the floor is ceramic tile, you may need to use a grout cleaner. It is best to check with a tile store to get the best instructions for cleaning and sealing tiles that are Stiletto, Mexican or other porous tiles. You can clean tile floors in sections as well as seal them in sections.

Wood floors may do well with a good waxing and polishing. However, you may need to refinish the floors. Ideally you will refinish wood floors by doing one complete room at a time. There is no rule that states that you cannot refinish a floor section by section. That is certainly better than not refinishing them at all. Which methods you use to refinish wood floors will depend on whether you will be refinishing them yourself or hiring them done.

If the floor covering is carpet, you also need to decide if you want to clean it in sections, or if you will clean one or several rooms at a time. If you feel you have accomplished a big job by getting this far, I suggest that you clean the carpet in sections as you go. This is a good idea if it is going to take several weeks to get the room done. It will also depend if you have access to a carpet cleaner that you can use anytime or if you must rent one or hire someone to clean your carpets.

Select the furniture: Keep a room looking tidy by allowing several feet of space between large pieces of furniture. Chose the pieces you want to go against the wall and clean those furniture pieces using whatever method needed. (See Suggestion and Cleaning Section)

If the furniture is wood and needs refinishing, it can wait if necessary. Ideally now is the time to do it. The goal is to have each wall section COMPLETE IN EVERY WAY once you have finished.

If there is a window, you have already washed it once with soapy water when you washed the wall. Clean it one more time with vinegar and water or a window cleaner. Squeegee the windows dry or use wadded newspaper, paper towels or a clean cloth to polish to a luster.

Clean the window covering. If the window coverings are drapes or curtains, they may need to be cleaned or washed. Check the cleaning instructions on the tag. You can also wash mini-blinds or vertical blinds. (See Suggestions and Cleaning section) If you are replacing the window coverings with new ones, install them now.

Be sure to clean the fireplace if there is one on this wall. (See Suggestions and Cleaning section)

Make a choice of two to three wall decorations for the wall and hang them in place once they are clean. A good rule to follow is to have no more than three wall decorations hanging on each wall. Two items are ideal. This varies if you have several small items to make a grouping. Please hang only one grouping per wall. With a grouping, one additional wall decoration is acceptable.

Please select your wall decorations carefully. Avoid sunburst clocks or wood ducks with metal wings that were popular in the fifties and sixties. You want your decorations to be of this time period. You do not have to spend money to have nice decorations that are in style. Mirrors and family pictures are always a good choice. You can always freshen up old picture frames with spray paint, using the colors that are popular now.

Place the cleaned furniture of your choice against the wall. If it is a couch, add clean throw pillows. I personally do not like the looks of blankets or Afghans on the back of the couch. However, when I decide to lie down for a nap or to watch television, I like to have a blanket that is easily accessible. I fold my blanket and place it out of sight behind the couch. My sister has an end table with a door that opens in which she hides her blanket. However, this in your home; you do what you please; it does not matter. **Clean and easy to keep clean, is your goal.**

If there is a chair in the section, be sure there is a table placed next to the chair. Select and clean the items you wish to place on the table. (The same THREE-PIECE RULE that applies to items on the wall applies for the number of items placed on furniture.)

Remember if you place plants on wood furniture; be sure there is a tray under the plant to protect the furniture from moisture. (A ceramic plate purchased at a yard sale is far better than using a pie tin.) Never place plants on electrical equipment. One spill or overflow of water and you will have to replace the electrical unit. No plant is worth buying a new television, VCR, or CD player.

CONGRATULATIONS
You have cleaned one wall section of your living room. Doesn't it look great? Don't you feel good? Your chest fills with pride, and then you ask yourself…"What about all this stuff I moved out of that space that is now sitting here in the middle of the room?" You must decide what you will do with the boxes and the pile in the center of the room *before you proceed or before you stop.* What can you throw away? Look at the items in the pile hard and long. If you plan to keep any of these items, what will you do with them? Make those decisions now.

Welcome back and again CONGRATULATIONS! You are doing a great job. Following through is very, very important when doing housework.

The section you cleaned may have taken a day, a week or a month or longer, but it is finally complete and it will now be easy to maintain. It is important that nothing be returned or placed in the newly cleaned section. Each day you must check to be sure that area remains uncluttered and pick up any items that find their way there. (Actually, it is better if the person, who cluttered, picks up his or her own items.) Occasionally vacuum the floor and dust the furniture. It will take only a minute or two a day to keep it looking as clean as the day you cleaned it.

With the center of the floor cleared you are ready to forge ahead. It does not matter if you continue to clean today, tomorrow, next week or next month. Some of you will have the desire to continue. Others may feel as if you are unable to stop until the entire house is completely cleaned. Possibly you are wondering when you will find time to get sleep or go to work or do anything else. Please, if you are having these types of feelings, *stop for the day.* **PERFECTIONISM has a hold on you.** This is exactly the kind of feelings we want to overcome. *Only then can we have peace in our lives.*

Some of you may feel proud of what you accomplished but on the other hand you may be looking at the rest of the house and feel defeated. Those of you, who are experiencing these feelings, also need to stop for the day.

Only the people, who feel they are up to starting work on another section, should continue cleaning. Then you must be willing to work on the new section continually and steadily, whenever you can schedule the time. For some, this will mean that you wash the ceiling one-day and wash the wall the next. On another day, paint the ceiling, then the wall, doing each step one by one. If you follow this type of schedule, *what will you get?* You are right. You will have cleaned another section. What will you get if you wait until you can do an entire room or house?

I can guarantee that you will get a "Big Black Cloud" that will follow you everywhere, reminding you constantly of unfinished chores.

If you can learn that housekeeping is a continual process and overcome the feeling that it must all be done at once, you will adjust your way of cleaning so that you will end up with a house cleaned to your satisfaction. This is why we want to first go through the house thoroughly so we can streamline the job at hand. The work will be a little tedious and believe me; boring but it will be worth it. Please stay with me on this.

When you are ready to begin cleaning again, select another wall section and clean it. Clean the third wall and then clean the final, remaining wall. Once you have cleaned the last wall, disposed of the pile that has collected in the center of the room. Remove the items left in the box labeled FRONT ROOM. Place them in the box that designates where they will go. Take the remaining cardboard boxes to their designated home. Wash and/or paint the center of the ceiling. Once you have finished the ceiling, wash or shampoo the center of the floor. **Whew.... You have finished this room.**

CONGRATULATIONS

You have reached another plateau. You have cleaned and streamlined an entire room. It looks great. Give yourself a big pat on the back. YOU DESERVE IT.

During all the time you were cleaning sections and disposing of articles, did you even imagine how nice it would look in the end? Think back. Remember the night friends dropped by and one wall was noticeably cleaner and sporting new paint? You quickly explained that you were trying a new way of streamline cleaning, by doing it sections at a time. Your friends may have looked at you strangely and wondered if you had lost your mind. Perhaps, they questioned you about this new cleaning method and you ended up sharing what you had learned about yourself and housekeeping.

Then there was that night you had a nightmare about dump trucks showing up at your house and dumping piles and piles of food on your front lawn. When you asked what it was? You were told that it was all the food you had to eat before you left this planet. It was mountains and mountains of food. You woke up in a sweat at just the thought of having to eat all that food. You knew that all the housework that you still needed to do had brought on such a nightmare. Did you stop to think that you have already eaten mountains of food and it didn't even bother you?

That is the same way you want to learn to clean house. Bit by bit, slowly and steadily.

The great thing in this world
Is not so much where we are,
but in which direction we are moving.
Anonymous

CHAPTER 12 <u>THE KITCHEN</u>

We began with the front room because this is usually the entrance to your home. Now we need to go to the busiest room in the house. Yes, you are correct. It is the KITCHEN.

Kitchen

Please do not panic and do not run. Most of all do not give a big sigh and slam this book shut. Instead, select SEVEN large cardboard boxes and SEVEN smaller ones. Label them as follows:

1. KITCHEN
2. GARBAGE
3. GIVE AWAY
4. DONATE
5. STORAGE
6. NOT FOR THIS ROOM
7. CAMPING (This box is needed only if your family goes camping.)

You can use the "select a wall method" for cleaning the kitchen only if you have a wall that is cupboard free. If you have such a wall, follow the previous instructions used for cleaning the living room

In the past, enamel paint was the paint choice for kitchen ceilings and walls because of their exposure to cooking grease. Enamel paint made kitchen cleaning easier. Today, using a good water-based paint with a semi-gloss finish will allow easy cleaning of your kitchen. It is still a good idea to use enamel on wood trim, doors, and shelves. The kitchen is a room in which you may wish to use some color. Use pastel wall paint, wallpaper or wallpaper trim, to add color to the kitchen. Since you spend so much time in this room, you want it to be bright and cheerful.

If you do not have a wall that is cupboard free, or once you have cleaned that wall, begin with the top cupboards.

Top cupboards

Open all of the top cupboards and study their contents. Pay special attention to any non-kitchen items that are in your cupboards.

Remove the contents from *one or all* of the top cupboards. As you empty the cupboards, you will separate the dishes from the ones that you only use *occasionally*. These will be holiday dishes, such as turkey platters, large serving dishes, chip and dip dishes. Store them all in one cupboard. Use a cupboard that is least accessible to you. I am short, so I put them in the cupboard over the refrigerator. Remember if you feel you will *never use* any of these dishes, put them in the appropriately labeled box.

Stack and count the table settings. Do you have twenty-four plates? How many times do you have twenty-four guests? If you do not have large numbers of guests often, keep only two or three plates each for the number of people in your immediate family. This same rule applies to the number of glasses you will keep. Store these extra dishes in your HOLIDAY CUPBOARD or place in one of the labeled cardboard boxes. Get them out of easy reach so you have to make an effort to use them. If you are a person who has trouble washing dishes, you should not have many dishes. This forces you to do the dishes when needed and eliminates the amount of dirty dishes you will have at one time.

Keep one or two more bowls than you feel you need to prepare a meal. Put extra bowls in the HOLIDAY CUPBOARD or in the appropriate cardboard box. The idea is to rid your cupboard of unused dishes and to clear up the clutter. If you have anything that does not relate to the kitchen, *remove it*. For now you can put it in the box labeled, NOT FOR THIS ROOM.

This is a good place to mention that knick-knacks in the kitchen are seldom a good idea. Cookie jars; cup holders, napkin holders, salt and peppershakers, potholders and towels will be the decorations in your kitchen. If you do have knick-knacks that tie into the theme of your kitchen, please restrict them to two or three items.

Once you have sorted the dishes and the cupboard or cupboards are empty, wash each one with warm, soapy water. If the dishes from the cupboard are dusty, wash them. If you wish, you may line the shelves with shelf paper.

I suggest that you do not use shelf paper that glues to the shelf. It is very messy and time consuming to remove later. I have often used the paper designed to glue to the shelf but held it in place with thumbtacks or staples. You can also hold the paper in place by cutting approximately one inch from the edges of the paper that covers the glue. This gives you a small strip of the sticky paperback to glue to the shelf. This will hold the paper in place and makes it a lot easier to remove later. You only have to remove glued shelf paper one time before you learn this lesson.

Wash the cupboard exterior, including the wall and ceiling above the cupboards. Wash the ceiling out several feet from the wall towards the middle of the room. If the cupboards are wood, use a wood soap. Follow the washing with a good rubdown with lemon oil to replace moisture in the wood. You can then polish the cupboards with a good wood furniture polish to get rid of any oil marks left from the lemon oil.

You may want to hold off painting the ceiling above the cupboards for now. If you decide to paint the ceiling now, turn to "Painting the Ceiling" later in this chapter.

Painting kitchen cupboards

If the kitchen cupboards are wood with bad scars, nicks, splits or cuts, it is unlikely that wood soap, lemon oil, and furniture polish will make them presentable. If you decide to paint them, follow the wood preparation and painting information on the enamel paint can. Remember that you can paint one cupboard at a time if so desired. Do not make it a bigger project than you feel that you can handle at one time.

If the cupboard exteriors are a type of Formica, you can cover the exteriors with various washable wallpapers or contact paper. You may also be able to replace the drawer and cupboard fronts with new ones. Ask about the process at your nearest do-it-yourself store or talk with a handyman. Any cabinetmaker can give you suggestions and of course, prices.

Bottom cupboards

Next you will clean the bottom cupboards. Open all the doors. Take a visual inventory. Separate items that need to go into your HOLIDAY CUPBOARD. Remove anything unrelated to the kitchen and place in the appropriate place or cardboard box.

Cooking utensils

Remove cooking utensils from the cupboards. Do you have more utensils than you will ever use? If you have Gram's old cooker but have never used it, put it in the proper cardboard box. Old pans that you never use or need replacing are great for camping. Wash the cupboard interiors and put the cleaned utensils back into the cupboards.

Canned and stored food items

Remove all canned and packaged items. Clean the cupboard interiors. Discard anything that has passed the expiration date or anything that has been opened for a while. They may contain pests. Place any item that you know you will never use into the proper box.

Bulk items

Items such as sugar, flour, spaghetti, and rice, need to be in canisters, jars, or plastic containers with tight-fitting lids to protect them from moisture and bugs. This is the time to store your food in the correct containers. (Plastic containers are very inexpensive at most grocery and hardware stores.) It is best to keep your bulk items, canned goods and stored items in one area for easy access.

Once you have sorted your food items and placed them back in the clean cupboards, you will wash the exterior of the cupboards. Wash several feet of the floor in front of the bottom cupboards out towards the center of the room. Be sure to clean the toe area under the front of the bottom cupboards.

The toe area

The cupboard toe areas get a lot of abuse. Cover scared wood in the toe area with paint. Use semi-gloss black enamel paint. Flat paint is impossible to keep clean. Carefully use masking tape to tape around the cupboard and floor to keep the paint where you want it and to be sure you have a neat paint line. If the toe area is damaged to the point that you are unable to paint, you can apply a new board to the front of the cupboard. Remove all of the old board first. Any lumberyard can help you in getting the right type of board. I suggest that you stain or paint the board black, before you install it.

Under the sink

As a rule, people keep cleaning products under the kitchen sink. If you have small children or if small children ever visit your home. **NEVER STORE CLEANING PRODUCTS OR CHEMICALS OF ANY KIND UNDER THE SINK**. Store them in the cupboard OVER *THE SINK*. Most people keep drinking glasses in this cupboard. However, there is no Cupboard Police Patrol that will inspect and fine you if you do not follow that *unwritten* rule. Children's lives are more important. Even if a child is able to climb up on the counter, they will have difficulty standing on or in the sink to reach the cupboard. If you have children who are climbers, **place a lock on this cupboard**. You will also want to designate a top shelf in a kitchen cupboard for all medicine products. **This cupboard must have a lock**.

Please do not feel that you know your child so well that he or she would never get into the chemicals or medicines. One moment of curiosity can be fatal. Give yourself some peace. Lock up these items. This protection allows you to accidentally fall asleep on the couch for a few minutes when you are not feeling well. You can rest, knowing that your toddler or young child cannot decide to get some medicine to make mom feel better, tasting the medicine first. These types of accidents occur when parents are not up to snuff. It is very important that we store *all* our chemicals and medicines safely. I can guarantee that one day a child will be in your home, if for only a moment. Remove the possibility of that moment becoming a dangerous one. Please do not give yourself a false security by simply placing a childproof lock on this cupboard. Install a locking mechanism. Never under estimate what a child is capable of doing.

I remember when my oldest daughter was about two years old; the first childproof lid came out for baby aspirin. (We gave our babies' aspirin back then.) The cap was hard rubber and I could break a fingernail trying to remove it. I would finally resort to prying the lid off with a kitchen knife. What a chore it was to get the safety cap off when the baby was sick and I was half-asleep.

One day when my husbands' parents were visiting, we showed them the new safety cap. To demonstrate how safe it was, my husband handed the bottle to my two-year old and asked her to take the lid off for him. She tried to turn it a couple of times. Then put the cap in her mouth and removed it with her teeth, much as a man would remove a beer bottle cap, before the twist tops were popular. If you are unable to figure out how to do something, ask a child to do it for you.

Clean the cupboard under the sink and line with shelf paper if desired. This cupboard is a great place to store canned goods or pots and pans. Wash the exterior of the cupboard and the floor in front of the cupboard. Paint the toe space if needed. Rub the cupboard front with lemon oil and polish with wood furniture polish, or paint if necessary.

Drawers
Dump contents of drawers onto a counter or table. (Do not dump them all at once, unless you are up to it.) Wash the drawer, paying attention to the outside of the drawer sides. Rub the finished wood with lemon oil and polish with furniture polish. Line the drawer if you wish. Separate the non-kitchen items and place in the correct boxes. Toss or give away any items of which you have excess. Remember to put items in your CAMPING BOX if you have one. Return the items to the clean drawer or drawers.

Designate a coupon drawer
I find that almost everyone has a coupon drawer. I seldom use coupons myself, yet I have a drawer in which I keep coupons. I am famous for putting coupons in this drawer with the full intention of using them. I will, on occasion, even get a coupon into my purse. However, it will often disintegrate before I can remember to use it. I admire people who use coupons, even if only on occasion. Your choice of keeping your coupons organized and how to do it is entirely up to you. (Just imagine how nice it will be, when the family decides to order pizza and you are able to walk directly to the coupon.)

The goal here is to make a home for coupons and make sure to round them up daily and place them in this drawer. This means that you *will not* toss coupons in any other drawer or any other place in the house. When collecting coupons or cutting them out, walk to the drawer or your purse and put the coupons in their proper place. Then walk to the garbage and throw away the cuttings. Now, where will you put the scissors?

Designate a junk drawer

A junk drawer is a place for items that have no designated home or for items that are often needed. For example: the junk drawer will always house a screwdriver because you hate to walk to the garage, or basement every-time you need one. There will also be items such as scissors, batteries or a light bulb for a flashlight. The flashlight itself may be in the drawer. The drawer will contain an array of items, such as, ties for the garbage bags to small pieces of things that have fallen off or broken off something. (You place these broken parts here so you will know where to find them when you decide to fix the broken item. Remember to mark each item, stating where it came from or where you found it, because, believe me, you will not remember later.) *Everyone* will have at least *one junk drawer* and there are usually one or two in the kitchen. Please keep your junk drawers limited…**or they all become junk drawers.**

The junk drawer is often a halfway house for items from the kitchen counter, until you can get it to its proper home. This is especially true if you need to clean or prepare a meal in a hurry and cannot take the time to deliver items from the counter to their proper place. It is like the cardboard box marked NOT FOR THIS ROOM. Remember every couple of days; check the junk drawer and deliver things to their rightful resting-place.

Counter-tops

Clear the counter-tops of everything. Put anything left over from the cupboards or drawers in the proper box. The microwave oven, blender, toaster, cup rack, napkin holder, canister set, cookie jar, telephone and possibly a pencil holder for the phone and a note pad, are the items that remain on the counters. Thoroughly wash the countertops with warm, soapy water and any spray cleaner. Remember to wash the wall under the overhead cupboards and the bottom of the top cupboard. (If the wall between the counters and the overhead cupboards need painted, paint them now, after masking the counters and cupboards carefully.)

Stains

It may be necessary to use a little scouring powder to erase the hard-to-remove stains or marks from the countertops. Sprinkle the powder on a stain and damped with water. After the scouring powder sits long enough to dry, it will usually lighten any stain. If necessary, scrub hard with scouring powder. I like to use a scouring powder that contains bleach. I have never been very good at pouring bleach on a stain and allowing it to sit. It seems that I end up with the bleach on things other than the designated spot, like my clothing. Scouring powder stays put without running someplace I don't want it to go. As a rule you will try to avoid harsh cleaners for your countertops, but occasionally, you may have to resort to harsh methods. Rinse thoroughly once the counters are clean. Polish with an appliance cleaner for that final spit and polish look, which also makes wiping up future spills a lot easier. For ceramic counters see the (Suggestions and Cleaning section)

Clean all items that will remain on the kitchen counter

Small appliances

Use warm, soapy water to clean small appliances and always **BE SURE THAT APPLIANCES ARE UNPLUGGED WHEN CLEANING.** Never use abrasives when cleaning small appliances with metal finishes. They will mar the finish. As a rule, most surfaces will clean with soap and water, a spray cleaner and a toothbrush. I find that when toasters and other appliances refuse to clean with soap and water, a light rubbing with water soaked, soaped up, scouring pad will do the trick. If you rub hard, you will scratch the finish, but if you use a light stroke, it will remove baked on residue with little effort, without damaging the surface. You may want to be careful using spray cleaners on painted numbers. I have seen numbers removed from washing machines and stove knobs by spray cleaners. Perhaps the products have improved but I suggest that you do not take the risk.

Microwave

The microwave has flat surfaces, inside and out and usually the plastic protected control panel that clean easily with soap and water. You may have to wet the inside of the oven thoroughly and let it soak to loosen the splatters on the ceiling and walls. You will also need to soak any food that boiled over on the bottom of the oven. If the exterior surface of your microwave is a fake, wood-like finish, it may only need to be dried with a towel after cleaning. You can use a window cleaner to clean the see-through door. During cooking, if you place a paper towel in the oven bottom, you will be able to clean up cooking spills easily.

Blender

The blender is a hassle when it comes to cleaning. The buttons are usually close together, making it impossible to get your fingers between them for cleaning. Cotton swabs are great for these areas as well as a toothbrush. If you use a toothbrush, make sure that it is slightly damp; you do not want water to get into the button mechanism. I also find that toothpicks are great for cleaning hard to reach crevices on the blender. Most blender pitchers come apart for cleaning. Wash in warm, soapy water, reassemble and run the blender empty for a couple of seconds to dry the blades thoroughly. For quick cleanups, run the blender with the lid in place with several drops of soap and water to wash. Rinse the same way. Dry with a towel and run empty to dry the blades.

Toaster

The toaster has a tray that opens on the bottom to remove crumbs. Clean this tray with a damp cloth. If you feel the need to clean it more thoroughly, use a soapy scouring pad. **Remember to unplug the toaster before cleaning.** Once the toaster is clean, polish it to a high polish with a dry towel. You can use a spray window cleaner for that squeaky-clean polish.

This is also a good place to advise you that you should never place toasters on a low shelf or utility cart that children are able to reach. Not only will they place things in the toaster, but also I once read about a toddler who kissed his own image in the toaster and was electrocuted. It was a defective toaster, but please keep appliances out of the reach of children.

Counter items

Clean all other items that reside on the counters, such as telephones, cup racks, napkin holders, knick-knacks, salt and pepper shakers, cookie jars and canisters.

Once you have washed your shakers and canisters, it is a good idea to allow them to dry for *several hours or overnight* before re-filling. The containers may appear to be dry when you add the contents. However, if there is the slightest moisture remaining, the next time you open the containers, the food will be lumpy or caked inside. If you wash canisters, jars or cookie containers that will remain empty for a while *do not put the lids in place for several days.* Putting lids on freshly cleaned containers will cause them to smell musty or allow mold to grow.

Harsh is a memory of trying to help my husbands' grandmother *by cleaning her house for her* while she was on vacation. I washed her "clown" cookie jar and replaced the clown's lid hat. When she returned several weeks later, she was unable to remove the moldy smell. Even soaking the jar in bleach and other cleaning products did not work. We could not save the jar. The flowers that later grew in that cookie jar haunted me every time I visited her home. As you can see, I have guilt connected to a lot of my housecleaning escapades. Avoidable guilt, if I had only…MINDED MY OWN BUSINESS.

Can you believe it? **THE CUPBOARDS ARE FINISHED**. Isn't it amazing? You are able to see how neat the cupboards are inside, even though closed doors? It is as if you have X-ray eyes.

With the small appliances cleaned, we will now graduate to the dreaded, LARGE appliances.

The range hood

The range hood will be one of two kinds, vented or non-vented. The hood is usually mounted under a cupboard or it could be under a mounted microwave oven. In any case the cleaning is the same. There will be a light fixture with a glass covering. Remove the glass and clean. Fasteners hold this glass in place or the glass will slide or lift into place. You will discover which it is by trial and error. You may wish to remove the light bulb as well to avoid breakage if sprayed with cleaner or splashed with water.

The hood may also have a filter. Often you can clean the filters in hot, soapy water and reuse them. Sometimes you can even clean a charcoal filter a time or two before replacing. If you decide to clean the charcoal filters, use ONLY HOT WATER. Soaps may cause a reaction with the charcoal and produce tiny growths that resemble small cauliflower heads. Later, when you turn on the blower, these little popcorn-like pieces will spew out of your vent, into your food.

Once you have removed the light bulb, glass and the filter, scrub the underside surfaces of the vent with any method that works. I like to spray the surface with spray cleaner, and let it sit awhile. Then follow up by using a soapy scouring pad. Avoid spraying cleaners on any electrical wires or connections. Also avoid these same areas when using a *metal scouring pad.*

I like to give the cleaned surface a protective coat of appliance polish after cleaning. Replace the new or cleaned filter, light bulb and the glass.

Wash and clean the exterior of the range hood, which includes the control panel. Polish with appliance cleaner and buff with a dry cloth. The range hood often has a painted surface, but is not baked on like the top of the range. Scouring powders or pads will scratch or remove the paint. If the surface is unpainted metal, such as brass or stainless steel, use the proper cleaner and follow the instructions.

The range

It will not matter what kind of range you have. You can usually pull both the built in and the free standing range, from the wall. **Be careful not to stretch the electrical cord or gas line**. The length of the gas line will limit the distance that you can move a gas range. You can usually unplug an electric range and completely removed the range from its spot. If you are unable to reach the plug-in from behind, or above, remove the bottom drawer. You might be able to reach the plug under the stove. Pulling the range out from the wall will allow you to get behind the range to clean. Before you clean the range itself, clean behind it.

Wash the walls and cupboards surrounding where the range sat, including the back of the range and the floor. If you are limited on how far you can pull the range from the wall, you will only be able to clean as far as you can reach. Using a large, soapy sponge, wash the walls and the back of the range. This is when a sponge mop comes in handy. Using the mop, scrub the walls and floor. You can also drop a soapy rag on the floor and use a broom handle to move it around on the floor to clean. Use the broom handle to pick up the rag once you finish. If the wall needs painted, paint it now, even if you are only able to reach part of the wall. Once you clean and paint the range area, polish the cupboards and the floor.

Remove the rings, burners and drip pans from the top of the stove. If the burners do not remove, lift them to remove the drip pans and rings. (Place the drip pans and rings in a sink full of hot, soapy water to soak.)

If the top of your range lifts for easy cleaning, raise and prop it open. Using plenty of water, soak up and remove all spills. For stubborn spots, you can use a scrub sponge or scouring pad. If the stovetop does not lift up, reach inside the burner openings and clean the drip area. If you must do this to clean the drip area, it is a good idea to **UNPLUG THE RANGE**, because you will be using water around the wires to the burners. If you are unable to unplug the range, use only a damp sponge or cloth to clean, avoiding all wiring. (Do not use a metal scouring pad around electrical wires.) When cleaning gas ranges, be sure that you do not put out the pilot light. If you find that you accidentally put out the pilot light, **light it again-immediately**. You may have to refer to your range booklet for instructions on lighting the pilot light, if the instructions are not printed on the range. You may have to call for instructions. Call the gas company, repair shop, or the landlord.

Once the drip area is clean, dry the cleaned surface with paper or cloth towel and close the stovetop. Wash and dry the top of the range. Use a toothbrush, cotton swab, or toothpicks to clean around the control panel. You can remove the range knobs and soak for a short time, in soapy water. Long soaking may remove the printing on the knobs. Polish the range top with appliance polish, and rub to a luster with a clean dry fabric towel or cloth.

The same cleaning procedures apply to a range top built into the counter.

The oven—Self-Cleaning

If your oven is self-cleaning, you will follow the instructions from the manufacturer. The instructions appear on the inside of the oven door or below the control panel on the top of the range. It is a good idea to clean up any bad spills and remove any large food particles from the oven before engaging the self-cleaning process. The oven is designed to burn off the spilled food, with a high degree of heat, to clean the oven. If you have bad spills or food particles, they will produce smoke.

I remember one time when the fire department came and carried my neighbors stove out of her house because it was smoking. Once the self-cleaning begins, the oven door will automatically lock and stays locked until the oven returns to safe heat levels. You can turn off the cleaning process, but you are unable to open the door and deal with the smoke.

You may leave the oven racks in the oven when using a self-cleaning oven. Since the oven cleaning instructions say to remove all utensils, it is not a good idea to clean the burner rings and drip trays in the oven. Once the oven has gone through the cleaning process, the oven door will automatically unlatch. Using a damp cloth, wipe up any ashes or residue from the cleaning. Line the bottom of your range with tinfoil, unless your range instructions advise against using foil in the oven. Replacing the foil after spills will keep your oven sparkling longer. Never cover racks with foil. Foil will hinder the heat flow of the oven.

Burner drip pans and rings

Badly burned or scarred stovetop drip pans and rings can be easily replaced. You can purchase them at any hardware store. Cleaning can be tedious, but not impossible. I personally am a great user of scouring pads. Using a *"light touch"* method will easily clean the presoaked rings of cooked on food without scratching the ring's surface. Use only soapy water to clean burner rings. Oven cleaners may dull or tarnish the chrome.

For easier cleaning the next time, you may be able to cover your drip pans with foil. Never cover the center hole on the drip pan that covers the "oven vent". You also have the option of using a cold oven cleaner to spray your drip pans for easier cleaning.

The oven-Conventional

If you are the owner of an oven that will not clean itself, you get to use oven cleaner. There are several on the market and you will discover which ones you like best. There are oven cleaners that you spray on a warm oven and wait a short time and ones to spray on cold ovens and leave all night. If you feel that you may find yourself "putting off" cleaning the oven, I suggest that you use the cleaner that you spray on a warm oven. Personally, I find they both work quite well. I just dread going to sleep knowing what waits for me when I awake.

Be sure to leave the racks in place and put the burner drip pans in the oven to be cleaned. Spray generously with oven cleaner.

Remove the oven cleaner as directed on the can. The foam will be moist for removal. If you wait until the foam dries, it is more difficult to remove. If you do forget and allow the cleaner to dry, use plenty of water to wash the oven. Do not make this job worse than it is, by exchanging a dirty oven for a dirty oven coated with dried cleaner.

Follow the instructions on the can for rinsing the oven after removing the cleaner. Line the bottom of the range with foil if desired.

Anytime you use oven spray cleaners, be sure to properly ventilate the room, and **avoid breathing the fumes**. You may want to turn on your range hood vent during spraying.

Remove the oven door

Before removing the oven cleaner, check to see if your oven door removes. To remove the door, open the door until it catches at the first notch. Firmly grasp the door, on the sides, and lift. Be careful to keep the door aligned with the open hinges. If you fail to keep everything aligned, the door may bind and you will have to push the door back in place and start again.

Once you remove the door, avoid any contact with the hinges, if you bump them they will snap closed, like alligator jaws. **If you or a small child has your fingers in the way, there may be a serious injury**. I always push the hinges so they pop into a closed position until I am ready to replace the oven drawer. *Messing with these hinges is very much like setting a mousetrap.* When I am ready to replace the oven door, I use a kitchen towel to pull the hinges into the open position. I hold the towel ends, loop over the hinge and pull, until the latch is in position. This way, if it does not catch in position and snaps shut, my fingers are not readily available to be smashed.

Set the oven door aside. Be very careful that you do not rest the oven door where it will be knocked over and hurt a child or pet, or where it may fall and break the oven window. With the door removed, you have easy access to cleaning and/or rinsing the oven.

The bottom of your range

Often the freestanding ranges on the market now have no pan drawer or broiler located below the oven. I think it is a terrible decision to do away with the pan drawer in the range. Your range may have a drawer or a broiler located below your oven. If you have a broiler, it is possible to clean it with one of the cold spray oven cleaners. Let it sit for a while. Wipe clean, with paper towels and wash with hot, soapy water. If you wish, you can clean the bottom of the broiler pan, by placing it in your oven when you use the conventional oven cleaner. However, the oven cleaner may discolor the broiler chrome grill.

If you have a drawer, remove it so you can clean it thoroughly at the sink or bathtub. If you were unable to pull the range out from the wall, removing the drawer will allow you to reach under the range and clean the floor. Wash and clean all remaining parts of the exterior of the range. Polish with appliance cleaner and buff to a luster with a clean cloth. Push the range back into place and plug it into the wall socket.

Refrigerator

Unplug and pull the refrigerator from its resting spot. This is easy, if your refrigerator has wheels. If not, you may want to consider purchasing wheels or discs that easily slip under your refrigerator. They are very inexpensive and can be purchased at any hardware store. These aides for moving heavy items are also great for anything else you may need to move, such as other appliances, trunks, heavy boxes, or even heavy planters. (You may need help in tipping the appliance to put the wheels in place.)

If your refrigerator has a waterline, be very careful when moving the refrigerator. You must avoid pulling or bending the waterline. This may be a good time to change the water filter.

Once you have moved the refrigerator out of its spot, wash the walls, underside of the cupboard, back of the refrigerator and the floor. Paint the wall if necessary and polish the floor.

If the waterline prevents you from removing the refrigerator completely from its spot, you will still be able to reach most wall and floor areas that need cleaned. If you are unable to reach all areas, clean with a sponge mop, like you cleaned behind the range.

Remove all food from the freezer. Sort the food. Throw away anything that has been in the freezer more than a month, unless it is an item that you are sure you will be using soon. Place items you wish to keep, in a picnic cooler or a large box, or place in large cooking pots. Put ice from the ice trays, or the trays themselves on top of the frozen food to keep it from thawing.

Remove everything from the refrigerator. Sort the food; getting rid of old food or food that you know you are never going to use. How long have you had that last inch of mustard in the jar? Throw it away. Do you really need those packets of catsup from McDonald's? Remove the drawers and shelves. If necessary, place the refrigerator racks and drawers in the bathtub to soak.

If you have a freezer that requires manual defrosting, do that first. It can take a freezer a long time to defrost on its own. You can speed up the defrosting by placing a warm pan of water in the freezer. I have read that closing the freezer door speeds this process. I have found that it works better with the door open. It seems as if the warm outside air helps the defrosting process. It just appears to take a lot of hot water to totally warm up a closed freezer.

Replace the cold water with new warm water, until defrosting is complete. You may also pour warm water over the ice as it begins to melt. If you are impatient and wish to begin prying the ice loose with a kitchen knife, be careful not to puncture the walls of the freezer or cut or break any pipe or tube lines. You will leave scratch marks if you use a metal knife, so take that into consideration, before you do it.

I have heard of people using a hairdryer to defrost a freezer. However, *I have a problem with using an electrical appliance when there is a good chance that there will be water on the floor where I am standing.*

Using dish detergent, wash the interior of the freezer and refrigerator with warm, soapy water. Avoid using cleaners that contain pine or other strong scents that may linger in the refrigerator. There is nothing less desirable than eating butter or drinking milk or soda that tastes like pine trees. Just think, pine tree ice cubes. Yukkk. If there is a bad odor, use vinegar or baking soda in your rinse water, and place the remainder of the opened, unused box of baking soda in the refrigerator after cleaning. The baking soda will absorb the odors in the refrigerator. Discard the box of baking soda after a couple of weeks and replace for a new one for continued odor protection.

If I leave the refrigerator plugged in during cleaning and turn it off at the controls, I remove the light bulb. Once water hits the warm bulb, it burns out or breaks.

Pay close attention to cleaning the rubber around the doors. They have grooves that are famous for collecting crumbs. Also be sure to wash the underside of the doors, where spills love to lurk. A toothbrush may come in handy for grooves on the freezer door or the door rubber.

Once the refrigerator and freezer are clean, replace the clean racks, drawers and food. Plug in the refrigerator, or turn on at the controls. Fill your ice cube trays with clean water.

Wash the exterior of the refrigerator and polish to a high gloss with an appliance cleaner. Push the refrigerator back into place. (Watch closely not to bend the waterline if you have one.)

At this time, select the items to place on the front of the refrigerator. Often children's artwork hangs on the front of refrigerators. If you set rules about how long a picture will remain on display and set guidelines on requirements for the artist to get the right to display their art, you will accomplish two things.

First it will keep the refrigerator looking neat. Second, it will add excitement for the artist to know that their art showing is specifically for them. Without rules you may find anything displayed from catalog cutouts to anything the young artist feels belongs there.

I found that a bulletin board works for family members to display any and all items of interest. I kept the refrigerator for the one or two drawings by a special artist. Each family member had a designated week in which they could display the art or item of interest that they wished to share. If they came home with a really great picture and it was not their week for display, they could still show their art on the bulletin board. When their display week arrived, it then took the prestigious place of honor.

Watch for the special showing by a child who displays his or her art when it is not their week. Siblings will often allow a brother or sister to show their project out of sequence. The child who gives this special permission or relinquishes his or her refrigerator space gets pride in doing so. If you are comfortable with an *anything goes attitude*, when it comes to your refrigerator front, then go for it. If you have magnets or potholders that attach to the refrigerator, be sure they are clean before reapplying to the freshly cleaned appliance.

Dishwasher

The great thing about a dishwasher is it cleans itself, but it does need help with its exterior. Wash with warm, soapy water, paying attention to the control panel, using a toothbrush, cotton swab, or toothpick to get into tight areas. Polish with appliance cleaner and buff to a luster with a dry, clean cloth. If the lower front panel of the dishwasher will lift out, you can vacuum the dust from under the dishwasher. You are then able to use a damp cloth and wipe the floor under the unit.

If the dishwasher has an odor, you can place a small bowl of water and bleach in the bottom of the dishwasher. The incoming water will cause the bowl to run over, allowing the diluted bleach to circulate throughout the appliance. You can follow the bleach with a vinegar rinse, using the same method.

Light fixtures

Using a ladder or chair, remove all light fixture glass. Be sure that you have the light fixture turned off long enough to cool before removing. Use warm, soapy water to wash and clean the fixture, also washing the ceiling around the fixture. **Be careful to avoid all electrical wires**. Place the light fixture glass in the dishwasher or carefully wash them by hand in the sink. Pay attention to the cut edges of the fixture. You can easily cut yourself on these edges. Rubber gloves are good protection from cutting yourself and will allow easy grip on wet glass. If the glass is too large to wash easily in the sink, you may need to wash them in the bathtub. Place towels in the bottom of the sink or tub to help prevent breakage.

Once the fixtures are clean, use a sponge mop to finish cleaning the ceiling. You washed the perimeter of the ceiling when you cleaned the cupboards and the cupboard-free wall. Then you cleaned the ceiling around the fixtures when you washed the fixtures. That does not leave a lot of ceiling left to clean. However, do not put the light fixture glass back in place, until you have finished washing and/ or painting the ceiling. Never trust yourself around glass when flailing a sponge mop or paint roller around in the air.

Paint the ceiling

If the ceiling needs painting, you may have already painted the ceiling over any cupboard-free walls that exist in your kitchen and around the light fixtures. However, you may have elected to wait to paint above the cupboards. It is always a good idea to mask around wood cupboards and tape plastic drop cloths over the cupboards before painting near them. Paint dropped on wood cupboards may not clean up well and you may end up with white paint marks embedded in the wood. Also cover the floor with plastic drop cloths. Use an extension to your paint roller to paint the ceiling. If you will be painting the walls, paint down a couple of inches on the wall. If you are painting only the ceiling, be sure to have a neat paint line connecting the ceiling and wall. After the ceiling is painted, replace the cleaned glass to all light fixtures.

Finish up

Once the walls and ceilings are washed, clean and painted, it is time to remove the labeled cardboard boxes and clean the floor. Take the boxes to their proper location. Ideally, the GIVE AWAY box, anything designated for other family members, goes in the trunk of the car and the donation box goes by the back door or to the garage, to await delivery. This is a great time to enroll other family members in helping to distribute and empty boxes. You may set aside the box labeled, NOT FOR THIS ROOM, *as long as you empty it before continuing to the next room.*

Use whatever method is required to clean the floor. Since you cleaned the perimeter of the floor already, around the cupboard-free wall and the cupboards, you only have the center of the floor left to clean. (See Cleaning and Suggestion section if needed.)

Congratulations

You have cleaned the room in the house that **I dread most of all**.

This is a good time, to remind you. **You do not have to do all this work in one day.** Keep telling yourself to do only what you feel comfortable with doing. If you clean one cupboard a week, what will you have in a month? That's right. You will have four clean cupboards. You now have four clean cupboards that you didn't have a month ago.

Like any room in the house, it may take several or many days to complete this room. Possibly you did one cupboard a night after the children were in bed, or you cleaned part of an appliance every other day or so. Maybe, you washed a wall, then on another day washed a window. You may have carried those cardboard boxes in and out so many times you cannot remember how many. You did it so you would not have to walk around them when you were not using them.

Did you apply a little pressure to yourself, to keep yourself on track and keep you moving towards your goal? Don't conjure up that "Black Cloud" to follow you around. Instead, see yourself as the sunlight that is breaking through those black clouds. Do a little something every day. In the end, the job will be complete. Housework is like writing this book. As long as I keep writing a page or two every day or so, eventually, I will have written enough pages for a book.

Please accept that once you clean a cupboard it will stay that way for some time. They will stay clean longer, because you now have less clutter in your cupboards. All the cupboards do not have to be cleaned at the same time. You will always *make progress* any time you do anything. Always compliment yourself on your accomplishments and be *accepting* of your compliments.

If you discover those old feelings creeping back into your life, go over the paperwork or the tapes you made during **The Exercise**. Get back to the understanding you had at that time. Remember to share with relatives and friends what you are doing. When people know what direction you are heading, they understand why one wall has paint of a different color.

Keep in mind that the feelings you have about your housekeeping *are yours*. You learned this in **The Exercise.** Be proud of what you achieve. Do not fall back into feeling guilt about the way you keep house or do not keep house. If you have come this far in this book, you are doing great! Pat yourself on the back. Y*ou deserve it*. I told you that it might not be easy. Even if you are cleaning with gritted teeth, you will be doing maintenance cleaning with a SMILE. **I promise**.

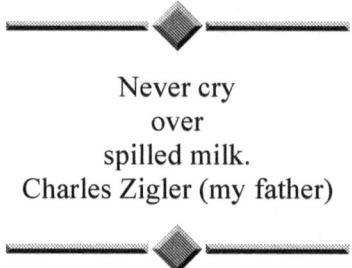

Never cry
over
spilled milk.
Charles Zigler (my father)

CHAPTER 13 THE BATHROOM

Let us go to the next place visitors may go while in your home. The
BATHROOM

Bathroom
Items you may need for this room:
Cardboard boxes
New shower curtains
New window curtains
Bathtub appliqué's
De-scaler cleaner
Plumis stone
Enamel paint, and paint equipment
This may be the SMALLEST ROOM in the house, but it may also be
the *most dreaded*. Reminding myself that it is the smallest **room** in the
house helps my attitude when it comes to cleaning the bathroom.

The medicine cabinet
First of all, medicines always need to be in a locked, top, *kitchen*
cupboard, out of the reach of children. Never keep medicines in the
bathroom. Moisture from showers and baths can damage medicine,
rendering it less effective. If you have medicines in the bathroom, sort them
now. Flush any old and unused medication. It is never a good idea to keep
unused medicine. (All medicines are to be totally consumed when
prescribed.) Medicine is usually out of date, or in a weakened state by the
time you need to use it again. Using medicine without a prescription is not a
good medical choice.

Walk immediately to the kitchen and place any and all medicines that
you plan to keep in a top cupboard that can be locked.

Remove the rest of the items from the medicine cabinet. If any of these
items do not pertain to the bathroom, place them in the appropriate
cardboard box.

Once you have emptied the medicine cabinet, remove the cabinet
shelves and any sliding cabinet doors. Wash the shelves and doors in warm,
soapy water in the sink or tub. (Always put towels in the bottom of the sink
or tub to help prevent breakage.) Wash the interior and exterior of the
cabinet with warm, soapy water. If the cabinet has attached or enclosed light
bulbs, be sure to turn off the light and let the bulbs cool before cleaning
around them. (This is a good time to take a five-minute coffee break.)

Use only a damp cloth to clean around the light bulbs and be sure to avoid getting any moisture in the outlets. **Never mix water and electricity.** Even a damp cloth against a hot light bulb will cause it to burn out or burst. Replace any burned out or defective bulbs and resume cleaning.

Wipe off or wash any items going back into the cabinet. These items will be the usual toiletries and makeup that frequent the bathroom. I know some of you are laughing when I mention putting makeup in the cabinet. If

you have a lot of makeup, toss it all in a woven or plastic basket. The basket can sit on the countertop or a shelf for easy access. You may even prefer to keep your makeup in a makeup bag and keep it under the sink. (Do not store makeup under the sink if you have small children or have small children come to visit.)

Under the sink and cabinet drawers
Empty the area under the sink and the cabinet drawers. Wash with warm, soapy water. Line with shelf paper, if desired. Rub wood cabinets with lemon oil and furniture polish or paint if needed. Clean and replace the items you wish to store in these places. **Remember** all chemicals and cleaning items belong up high in a childproof, locked cabinet in the kitchen or laundry room.

The tub or shower
If you have shower curtains, remove them at this time. If you plan to keep and reuse these curtains, fill the tub with very warm, soapy water and put the plastic liner or plastic curtains in to soak. If you have fabric curtains and plan to keep them, wash them in the washing machine now, so they will be clean when you are ready to hang them. Hang fabric curtains to dry. If you use the dryer for these curtains, *dry on very low heat.*

I usually wash plastic curtains in the bathtub, by hand, with a scrub brush. Once the curtains have soaked, I drain the tub of most of the water, leaving about one to two inches of water. Using a brush and a de-scalar type spray cleaner, I clean one side of the curtain, folding it as I go, until I have completely scrubbed the curtain or liner. I have found that putting plastic in the washer seldom works. The curtains fold and do not come clean in the folds. If you do decide to try to wash plastic curtains in the washer, be prepared to replace them if they tear into pieces. Use a towel to dry the plastic curtains or hang on a line to dry.

New plastic liners are very inexpensive, so if your liner looks discouraging, buy a new one, the same goes for plastic curtains. I personally like fabric shower curtains with plastic liners. I can change the liners whenever I feel cleaning it gets too tough or when I want a new color. I love being able to have fabric-ruffled curtains that I can wash when they get dusty.

To clean the tub and shower tile, you need a good tub and tile cleaner. Cleaners that remove scum, mold and water spots are the most desirable and less work to use. Spray the tile and the tub sides thoroughly with spray cleaner and let them soak for ten to fifteen minutes. **Do not spray the tub bottom at this time**.

Step into the tub to clean the tile. Wear good rubber shoes that will prevent you from slipping. **Do not become a statistic** on the list of injuries received during a fall in the tub. Bare feet are slippery and standing in the cleaning chemicals may irritate your skin.

Use a good scrub brush to clean the tile thoroughly. Use additional cleaner if needed. I personally like to use a carpet brush. It has a longer handle than most scrub brushes. I also use a powdered cleanser on the tile grout, scrubbing it in with a toothbrush. My favorite tool for cleaning tile is the net scrubber that people use in the place of a loofah sponge when they shower. (It is constructed of netting and gathered into a ball.) It is easy to hang on-to and when sprinkled with powdered cleanser, it is great for cleaning the ceramic tile surface and the tub. (Be sure to rinse the netting thoroughly, if you plan to use it on your body in a shower later.)

Once you have cleaned the shower and tub, you will need to decide if the tile needs re-grouting. This is the time to do it, if it needs it. Grouting is not difficult. You will use a grout tool to remove all loose grout and ready the other seams for grouting. Once you mix the grout, spread it on with a grout float and wipe off the residue grout, using a clean sponge. Seal with grout sealer and the job is complete. The biggest draw back to grouting is that you may have to keep the tile dry for several days to a week, while working on the tile and allowing for drying time. (For detail grouting instructions, attend a class at your local home maintenance center or obtain written instructions from a tile store.)

If you are not re-grouting at this time, you may wish to whiten the grout by spraying with a bleach-water spray. Use an old spray bottle. Fill the bottle one third of the way with bleach and fill the rest of the bottle with water. Be sure to cover any bathroom carpet with plastic drop cloths, before using the bleach-spray. Also remove any rugs, towels, or clothing, to avoid the bleach mist or-over-spray.

Spray the bleach mixture on the tile and grout as quickly as you can. Turn on the bathroom vent fan and /or open the window if you have one and LEAVE THE ROOM. (**Bleach mixed with other cleaning agents gives off poisonous fumes**, when inhaled can make a person sick or can cause lung damage.) Since you may have recently used a cleaner, do not take a chance that there may be any residue cleaner left on the tile. Leave the room. Let the mixture sit for fifteen minutes, then rinse thoroughly with warm water. (Be careful when removing the plastic drop cloths after spraying with bleach. Do not get it against your clothes or any other fabric.) You may want to use an appliance polish on the tile for that really clean shiny look that will resist water spotting.

Fiberglass enclosure

When cleaning fiberglass bathtub enclosures you will want to avoid using powdered cleansers; they may scratch the surface. Use a non-abrasive cleaner that is designed for cleaning fiberglass. Once cleaned, you may want to use appliance cleaner to polish to a luster. I had a male friend who used car polish on his fiberglass tub enclosure. It looked fantastic.

Shower door

Shower doors are also cleaned with tub and tile cleaners. I personally like to use a razor blade scraper and go over the glass after I have sprayed it with cleaner and allowed it to soak. Rinse and go over the glass one more time with a razor blade, to get off any spots you missed. Please, use a razor blade scraper that securely holds the razor blade. (Holding a bare razor blade to do anything is asking for a serious cut.) You will also need a toothbrush to clean the sliding door tracks.

Bathtub appliqués

If your tub has bathtub appliqués and they cleaned up well and you have not decided to paint or change the bathroom decor, keep them. If the appliqués need replacing, you will want to replace them now. Remove the old appliqués, with the razor blade scraper and clean the tub bottom thoroughly. Once you have cleaned the tub bottom, dry with a towel and let it sit to dry several hours before applying new appliqués. You must be sure the tub bottom is dry.

When putting on new appliqués, remember, although they are decorative; do not become carried away with your design. Be sure that your placement of the appliqués does not allow any large amount of space between them. If you have room for one bare foot, you have room for a slip and a fall. Once the appliqués are in place, you should be unable to step anywhere in the tub, without standing on some part of an appliqué.

The toilet

Fill a bucket with warm water. Quickly pour the water into the toilet. Pour the water as fast as you can without spilling onto the floor. This quick rush of water will force the water to flush out of the toilet, leaving it almost empty for easier cleaning. If the water does not flush out of the toilet on the first try, fill your bucket and do it again until it does flush.

Spray the inside of the toilet bowl with a good, strong toilet bowl cleaner, preferably one with a de-scaling agent. While the toilet soaks, use soapy water and clean the outside of the tank, toilet and toilet seat. Use a toothbrush to clean around the seat hinges and the bolt covers that bolt the toilet to the floor. This is also the time you wash the wall under, behind and around the toilet. This will include any neighboring cupboards and the floor around the toilet. Use lots of hot, soapy water.

Toilet seats are inexpensive. If the seat has stains or chips, replace it with a new one. To save you numerous trips to the hardware store, place a piece of newspaper over the toilet and draw a pattern the shape of the toilet. (Be sure to include the position of the holes to which the seat bolts.) Use this pattern to measure the new toilet seats at the store, to get the right size. The shapes of toilet seats vary greatly.

By the time you have cleaned the outside of the toilet, the cleaning solution has set long enough for you to finish cleaning the inside of the toilet. Use a stiff toilet bowl brush and scrub the toilet. Be sure to clean under the rim of the bowl. This is where mold and stains are worse.

You can spray any remaining stains with more solution. You can also remove any stubborn stains or marks by rubbing with a plumis stone. After cleaning the inside of the toilet, wipe the rim and flush.

You may place solutions in the toilet tank to help reduce water deposit buildup and to help deodorize your toilet. Please be sure to read the label closely and follow instructions for use.

Light fixtures

Turn off the bathroom lights and allow them to cool. (This is a good place for another five-minute break) Remove all the light fixture glass and wash in warm, soapy water. Place the fixture glass in a safe place until you are ready to put back in place. (Remember safety tips about handling fixture glass.)

Ceiling and walls

Before washing the walls, remove all electrical plug-in covers and soak in warm, soapy water. Place screws in a cup or glass to avoid losing them down the drain.

Often you can reach most of the bathroom ceiling by standing on a small household stepladder. Wash the ceiling, walls and windows with warm, soapy water, using a brush to clean the baseboards and edges of the floor.

Ceiling or wall fan

Remove the cover of the exhaust fan. Using a dry cloth wipe the blades and wires clean of dust. Remember if you decide to use a damp cloth to clean stubborn blades, avoid electrical wires. Wash the fan cover in warm, soapy water and lay it aside.

Paint

If you are going to paint the ceiling, do it now. This paint can be either oil based or water based enamel. For the best results and easiest care, you need to use enamel paint. (Enamel stands up to moisture better.)

After painting, replace the exhaust fan cover and put the glass back on the ceiling light fixtures.

Paint the walls next. Before you begin to paint, remove the shower curtain rod, if you have one. Turn the rod until it loosens then remove. The rubber pads for the rod may be stuck to the walls. Remove them carefully because you will be reusing them unless you are putting up a new rod.

Woodwork paint will last longer and wear better if painted with oil-based enamel. Once you have painted the walls, replace the clean electrical plug-in covers and the shower curtain rod. Put the clean or new shower curtain and liner on the rod before installing. Place the rod at the desired height and turn until firm. Remember to use the rubber pads. This allows a snug fit.

The floor

With everything else cleaned in the bathroom, the final step will be cleaning the floor. Use the proper method for the type of floor you have. (See Suggestion and Cleaning section)

Once the floor is clean and dry, you are now able to put the bathroom into final order. Clean the window, mirrors and glass doors with a window cleaner and polish to a luster. Hang the cleaned or new window curtains and put up fresh towels. Organize and place items on shelves, the back of the toilet and the counter. Put down any throw rugs, wastebasket and the weight scale. Distribute the cardboard boxes and their contents to the places where they belong.

CONGRATULATIONS, you have cleaned the smallest room in the house.

HOWEVER…if you have more than one bathroom in the house, those will be the next rooms you clean, before continuing any further.

Since you are at this point, one of two things has happened.

1.   You are the proud owner of only one bathroom.
2.   You are the proud owner of several bathrooms and…you have cleaned them all.

This compliment is a special one for those of you who cleaned more than one SMALLEST ROOM IN THE HOUSE…**YOU ARE DOING SO GREAT!** (Accept the compliment proudly. You deserve it.)

CHAPTER 14 THE LAUNDRY ROOM

The Laundry Room

Everyone will have a laundry room or area. If you have enough room, you can keep the ironing board there, standing and waiting for when you will need to iron that badly needed article of clothing at the last moment. The perfect room would provide you with several lines for hanging clothes and a rod to hang ironed clothes. This area may also house all the soaps and cleaning agents that are needed for doing laundry. Store them in a locked cabinet out of the reach of small children. Be careful if you decide to keep bleach in a cupboard or shelf over the washer or dryer. I have known of several instances where the bleach bottle was dropped, or vibrated off the shelf during a spin cycle, spilling all over clothes in and on the washer, dryer and floor.

This room is a real dust and lint catcher. In fact, it is the breeding place in the house for dust bunnies and any creatures that resemble them. If you wipe down the washer and dryer often and make a habit of always emptying lint filters with every load, this area will never get too dirty. (Failure to clean lint filters is the number one reason for the need of a repairman.) If you allow clothes to *collect* in this room, you will need laundry baskets and clothes hangers to keep the clothes organized. Ideally, you will bring clothes in to launder, then immediately take them back out again once they are clean.

This room will be easy to clean if it houses only items pertaining to laundry. You can quickly wash down and polish the appliances and wash the ceiling, walls and floor then paint if needed.

You will have the best laundry possible, if it originally comes from a clean room. A hanging plant, if you like them, does well in the laundry area. If you have a window, keep the glass sparkling for a cheery work area.

CHAPTER 15 <u>THE BEDROOM</u>

The Bedroom

For this room, be sure you have plenty of cardboard boxes.

Everyone has a different view about the bedroom. For some, it is their haven away from the world. It is a place where a parent of small children can slip away for a few minutes of peace and quiet. It may also be a place one family member retreats to when sports take over the television and most of the inhabitants of the home. It is a quiet place to be when you need to do some work. It is private place where you can talk to another family member

- The bedroom is the most versatile room in the home.
- It may feel cozy, like the den of a hibernating bear. It is a place to cuddle in private with your mate.
- The master bedroom is often off limits to all children and guests can enter only long enough to retrieve their coats.
- The bedroom is considered to be "personal property" by most people. Therefore, bedrooms often have a lot of rules that are established by the owner of that room.

People keep things in bedrooms that are seldom in other areas of the house. For example, this could be anything from guns, to money or jewels and valuables of all sorts. (The "valuables" may have value only to the dweller of the room.) For adults, these items can range from precious photo albums to coin collections or sports equipment. For children, it may be toys they do not have to share, the special rock they found and the money they save.

For most, the bedroom is a place where you can drop clothes when you undress in a hurry, or a place to put the laundry you do not have time to fold.

Disaster may very well take over the bedroom before you get it cleaned. You might become more overwhelmed by the bedroom than by any other room in the house. Bedrooms hold so much stuff that when you begin pulling it out it seems to begin to come out on its own. Instead of decreasing, the piles seem to get bigger. The path you may have tried to keep open to the doorway seems to keep closing.

When it comes to cleaning the bedroom, where do you start? The small room within the room is the best place to start. That is right, it is the...

Closet

You probably have as much stuff in your closet as you have in the bedroom. It can easily take as long to clean the closet as any full-sized room in the house.

If you are painting the closet, the ideal way *is to empty the closet,* paint, then put back the closet items you will be keeping. Unless you plan to spend more than a day doing this, you may decide to do the closet in sections.

One reason you may choose to clean your closet in sections is because you will need a lot of space to pile everything you remove from the closet. If you have an empty corner, this is one idea worth entertaining. The goal is not to mess up the bedroom so badly that you are unable to live with it until completed. You want to be able to clean in sections and in spurts if desired. Do not become overwhelmed and drag out that "Black Cloud."

If you plan to paint the closet ceiling, I strongly suggest that you remove everything from the closet. I would be hesitant to cover everything in the closet with plastic drop cloths and to trust it to protect my clothing. One missed step or dropped item could ruin clothing that would cost more than the time it would take to empty the closet. You can bet that disaster would come to the most favored or expensive item in the closet.

If you paint, **never use enamel oil-based paint in a closet**. Oil-based paint will not dry fast enough to get things back in the closet and it seems that it never really thoroughly dries. You may find items and clothing stuck in the paint on the shelves and the walls months down the line.

Wash the ceiling and walls with warm, soapy water and use water-based wall paint. If the clothes rod is wood and it has no scarring, leave it the natural wood. You can stain or varnish the rod, but sand it lightly first. If you paint the wood rod, it will mark easily with the clothes hangers. Shelf paper for the shelves is optional.

If you are not going to paint, you can slide the clothes to one end of the closet and wash the cleared end of the closet. You will need to clear the floor space for that area, so you can clean the floor too. However, if you are unable to slide the clothes far enough to see a wall to wash, this method is not going to work.

If unable to move the clothing, because you have too many clothes, you will need to sort clothing now, then wash walls when you have more room on the rod to slide the hangers.

Sorting clothes and shoes

Be very serious about sorting clothing. If you have clothing you do not wear, donate them to someone who will. If you keep your collection of clothes to *ones you actually wear*, you will find that you have plenty of room in your closet and it will be easier to keep clean. The same rule applies to shoes. Donate them. If you have not worn them in *a year*, you are not going to wear them.

Often storage items end up in closets. If the items you store in your closet are too important to have elsewhere in the house or storage, keep them there.

Bedroom drawers

As you did in the kitchen, dump only the amount of drawers you can handle at one time, or the number you have time to clean during each session. Always work at a speed that fits your schedule and your ability to get yourself to do it. After all, you do have a goal and to go forward is the way to reach any goal.

I suggest that the first drawer you tackle is the underwear drawer. Toss those items that are sub-standard, you know…the ones with holes and tears.

Clean all the remaining drawers, organizing as you go. Remove everything from the drawers that do not belong in the bedroom. If you have things that you feel may not survive outside the bedroom, designate a storage, keepsake, or miscellaneous drawer.

Once you have sorted and organized all the clothing and shoes, you have completed the biggest and hardest part of cleaning the bedroom. By now, the cardboard boxes from the bedroom are no longer confined to the bedroom. They have migrated out into the hall and are starting to travel down the hall. You may even be receiving complaints from family member about the boxes piling up in the hallway. If this happens, hand them a box and ask them to take the box or its contents to its rightful resting-place. Once that happens, you will not see or hear from that family member again.

NOW IT IS TIME, TO SELECT A WALL.

I suggest that you select the easiest wall. Once you have cleaned that wall's six-foot area, decide if you need to paint. (In smaller rooms, or rooms that are overcrowded, you may need to reduce your cleaning area to a three or four-foot area from the wall.)

Clean and or paint that ceiling and wall area. Clean the furniture, wall hangings, and items that will return to that wall area. Put everything in place and go to the next wall. By now you have the routine learned, if you are unsure, return to the pages in the front of the book, starting with the living room.

The bedroom is a room that it is easy to overcrowd with furniture and wall hangings. Look closely at the furniture you have in the bedroom. Is there ample space between each piece? Can you do without some of the furniture and items you have in your bedroom? Be sure that you are not using the bedroom as a storage place for furniture that has no home in the rest of the house. If you find that you are keeping furniture because it is still good, but it has no place in your house, sell or donate it.

If the pieces you have are antique or heirlooms, you can keep them in the bedroom. However, if they are not bedroom pieces, you may be able to find a way to work them into the other rooms in the house. Most decors, regardless of the period you chose, will accommodate an antique quite easily. I never let any furniture decor rules keep me from enjoying my favorite pieces of furniture.

I live in Arizona, so I chose a "southwestern theme" for my living room, dinning room, kitchen and bathroom. However, tucked under the stairs sits an upright Montgomery Wards 1940 radio that belonged to my parents. I put a glass dish shaped like a chicken and small flower arrangement on the radio and hung a small Monet' print on the wall.

At the top of the stairs, in my upstairs hall, I have a small antique child's desk, also from the forties, which belonged to me as a child. On the desk, I have placed a small chimney lamp and I hung a large painting of flowers on the wall over the desk.

If you seem to have trouble blending in your antiques, group them in a setting off to themselves, such as a corner, alcove or under the stairs.

I decorated my bedroom in an "old time country theme." A small country shelf hangs on one wall of my bedroom. It supports an old rocking horse, a bear, and a doll, which my younger sister, Anita, made for me, that has legs made from the buttons from my grandmother's button box. (The same buttons I played with as a child.) One bedside table holds my modern two-alarm radio but the other holds a glass chimney lamp, my grandfather's old wind-up "Ben" clock, and a miniature pitcher and bowl.

Next to my room of miniature doll furniture, displayed in an old fish aquarium, sits an antique wicker doll buggy and a porcelain doll. On the headboard of my waterbed, I display a calico kangaroo with a baby in her pouch, which my aunt made for me when I was a child.

In one corner of the room, I have a small four-inch corner shelf that displays, in a glass dome, a small teddy bear that my sister Dorsa crocheted. The room is a real mixture of all the things I love which fit quite well into a country, antique theme.

MY OFFICE IS A COLLECTION ROOM. Items of all eras live in this room. I have shelves of books, wood and metal filing cabinets. I have a typewriter, computer, scanner and printer. Other items are my grandmother's oak desk table and a child's antique clothes closet. There is a miniature captain's cabin on the beach, built by my son and displayed in a glass, fish aquarium. Oh, and I must not forget **my photo wall.**

THIS ROOM BREAKS ALL THE HOUSEKEEPING RULES. Out is the rule about room between the pieces; out is the rule about number of items on the walls. After all, it is a room that belongs solely to me and *I can shut the door and no one sees it*. However, since I have broken all my own rules, I try to go out of my way to be sure that I keep it neat and orderly. No amount of cleaning in my office takes away its junky look, after all it is junky, but I can live with it. It houses all the things I need for an office and it provides places for items that will not fit into the rest of the house or decor.

For some of you, the bedroom will be your room that follows no rules. Accept that this is OK.

Cleaning and painting the center of the bedroom ceiling

Once you have cleaned and painted all the ceiling and wall areas of your bedroom, you will have the job of washing and painting the center of the ceiling. Reaching the ceiling over a bed can often be a challenge. Most of the time, there is not enough room to move the bed so you must use a stepladder or stool to reach the ceiling. Be sure to cover the bed and surrounding furniture with plastic drop cloths.

If you have a conventional mattress, you can place an old quilt and plastic drop cloth over the bed and walk on the bed to do the ceiling. However, you will do better if you can place a large piece of plywood or particleboard on the bed before walking on the bed. The board gives you a sturdy place to stand.

With a waterbed, you will accomplish nothing by standing on a mattress filled with water. A large board that reaches from side rail to side rail and is strong enough to support your weight is a good way to go. (Be sure to watch your footing if standing on a plank.) Otherwise, your only choice is to stand on a stool beside the bed and reach the ceiling with a sponge mop and a paint roller with an extension handle.

Clean the bed, clean the floor and back out of the bedroom, admiring your handiwork all the time you are exiting. Doesn't it look great? It looks like a new room doesn't it?

Pat yourself on the back...FOR A JOB...WELL DONE.

Whatever you do, do not allow any boxes to remain in the hall. You must be sure that the hall is clear *immediately* after you complete the bedroom. After all, how long does it take to gather the family members together and hand out boxes? You may even want to establish a rule that all family members will be helping with cardboard box deliveries after every room you clean. It is their contribution to your goal of a clean and organized home. After all, your goal will benefit all members of the home.

When it comes to the bedrooms of other family members, they need to be doing the sorting and organizing of their own rooms. You can then help or oversee the major cleaning, if they are children. Teens are capable of reading and following this book.

CHAPTER 16 <u>THE OFFICE</u>

The office

This room is the room where most of the papers of the house reside. Not only do they reside here, but I honestly believe that they breed and multiply here too.

Even if you have a room similar to my office in which you decide to break all the housekeeping rules, keep in mind this room still needs to be thoroughly cleaned.

To begin...

I would start with an inventory of everything in the office or study. Open each door, drawer and filing cabinet. Make a mental note of where you have things, if you are good at that. If not, write notes. Begin cleaning in the closet. As you clean and stack and store office items, use the list you made during inventory to merge multiple collection places into one. You will need a stack of computer paper near your computer, but you do not need several places for reserved paper. Put all supplies in one place.

After you have cleaned the closet or closets, SELECT A WALL. If you have a tendency to pull out a file cabinet and then push it back after you have washed the wall, I suggest that you **DO NOT DO THIS**. This will only encourage you to convince yourself that you will *clean the file cabinet drawers later*. I am afraid that will not happen. Unless you have mastered a lot of self-control by now, I suggest that you clean each file cabinet as you go. How you organize your files is completely up to you, however, *clean them at this time.*

Photo wall

Previously, I mentioned the photo wall. Often people will select a wall in the home to put family photos. Mine is as I mentioned before, in my office. It is a wall that you cover with photos of all sizes, of all family members and friends of every age. I have pictures of my children and their families, from when they were babies to their present ages. I have pictures of them in special events or situations. I also have pictures of my parents, sisters and their families. I even have pictures of myself. It is a way of showing and enjoying all the pictures you love but do not want to place in albums. A photo wall is the only time you should break the THREE-ITEM RULE. Hang photos of all sizes, from floor to ceiling, wall to wall, in any design you prefer.

CHAPTER 17 SEWING, CRAFT, OR HOBBY ROOM

Sewing, craft, or hobby room

This room is as bad as the office or study to clean. Instead of papers, you have a collection of various items and projects. Like the office, you will have a strong desire to pull out the furniture to clean, and then push it back against the wall. You may try to convince yourself that you will later return to organize the drawers and its contents. Again, I will suggest that you clean each drawer and box as you go. In the "Suggestion and Cleaning section", you will see how you can later accomplish BYPASSING. Your goal right now is to get it all *clean and organized*. Remember to have a big cardboard box marked DONATION when cleaning this room. You will be throwing away junk that has no place in your life or house any longer. Be truthful with yourself. Are you really going to do that project? How long have you kept it, thinking you are going to do it someday?

I have found that this type of room stays organized longer than most rooms in the house. Perhaps it is because we are doing a lot of organized projects when we are in this room and it carries over into cleaning up and putting away.

Shoeboxes and cigar boxes are great ways to organize small items in this room. Label the end of each box clearly with their contents and stack in the closet. You can always find boxes for storage of these items at craft, hobby and fabric stores. Yard sales are the best place to go for storage units or empty jars. Baby food jars come in handy for storing beads, etc. Using a hot glue gun, the jar lids can be glued to the bottom of a shelf to hold jars in plain sight for easy viewing of the contents.

Try in this room, to have a place for everything. If YOU MUST HAVE IT, HIDE IT. This is a good motto for any room, but it is very important in a room that holds so much. Organize things so they are not piled in boxes around the room. My sister Dorsa, bought an old stereo cabinet, removed the stereo and had a fantastic piece of furniture in which to store her fabric and sewing items.

CHAPTER 18 <u>FIREARMS</u>

Firearms

If you decide to keep firearms in your home, please keep them in a locked cabinet or closet. For extra precaution, **keep the ammunition in a separate place**. Never fool yourself into thinking you can hide firearms from children. Thousands of children are injured or killed each year by guns that were supposed to be empty and guns that the parents thought were inaccessible to kids. Please do not allow your child or the neighbor's children to become a national statistic.

CHAPTER 19 BASEMENT ATTIC, STORAGE ROOM, SHEDS AND GARAGE

Basement, attic, storage rooms, sheds and garage

These areas offer great challenges, because they are the rooms that earn the title of **COLLECTION ROOMS**. Most large open areas, such as these, are for most of us the most unorganized rooms of all.

Basement and attic

Since the basement and attic are part of the house, they will be the areas to begin cleaning next.

These areas were bad enough in the beginning, but as you cleaned the house, you undoubtedly added items and boxes to these rooms, compounding the disarray. These rooms probably look worse than before you started this cleaning project.

If you have living quarters or bathrooms in these areas, *clean them first.* This will give you a beginning place. If you do not have living quarters in these areas, you may be unsure where to begin.

Because you may be extremely tired of cleaning, the challenge of these areas could be overwhelming. This is the point where you will find it very easy to quit. **PLEASE DO NOT STOP**. Pull yourself up by your bootstraps and forge onward. It does not have to be finished today. If going forward right now seems like too much, *take some time off.*

Take the kids to the park. Get a sitter and take a candlelight bubble bath while you listen to soft music. Go to the beauty shop. Meet a friend for coffee and talk. Compliment yourself on your accomplishments by treating yourself. Relax and enjoy the day. YOU DESERVE IT.

Do not wait for someone else to compliment you. It is unlikely; that family members will give you any praise, because they may be feeling ignored. They may feel that you have shown more interest in the house than in them. Possibly they feel that the only attention they received was when you needed help with cleaning or toting the cardboard boxes.

You may realize something that I learned years ago. You may tell yourself that you clean house for THEM (your family) but you do not. *You do it for yourself* and they get to benefit from it. However, do not expect them to be grateful, because there is a good chance that they won't be. This does not mean to hold any hard feelings against them if they do not seem appreciative. Probably, you are giving them a gift that never mattered to them anyway.

Years down the line, when you see how your children care for their own homes and raise their own children, you will feel their unspoken gratitude. It warmed my heart when I saw my daughter stop sweeping the floor in the middle of the kitchen to pick up the baby and play with him. (Remember that I had to have all my chores done first, before I felt I could play with my babies.) Thank goodness. My extreme housekeeping rules did not repeat themselves in my daughters.

Do not wait to compliment yourself, until you feel you are through cleaning. If you do, you *will never get praise from yourself.* Because, you will never feel it is FINISHED. Learn to live with accepting that everything will never all be done at once, and *that's OK.* Perfectionists practically kill themselves trying to get things done to the point they can feel it is COMPLETELY FINISHED. That is really sad, because even the perfectionist will never have it all done. They will always find one more thing that needs to be done. More or different flowers need planting, the car could use a waxing, the chimney needs cleaning, or the gutters need emptying. Save yourself from self-afflicted misery. Know that it is impossible. It is like chasing the pot of gold at the end of the rainbow. IT'S NOT GOING TO HAPPEN.

Besides, *what if you did get it all done.* How long would it last? Long enough for the kids to take off their shoes. Long enough for someone to answer the phone and write a note and leave the pen and paper on the counter. Long enough for someone to bring in the mail or newspaper and lay them down on a counter or chair.

I saw a woman on a television game show in the fifties. She said that she stripped and waxed her floors *every single day*. She admitted to locking her family out of the house, until she cleaned all the floors. The floors were only some of the things she did to the extreme with housecleaning, yet she felt compelled to repeat those chores *every day*. She would never be FINISHED. Once the family stepped on the floor, it was dirty again.

If your housework were truly FINISHED, what would you do? Sit in the living room with your feet up and sigh, *"IT'S ALL DONE."* Then pray for the power to freeze-frame everyone, so it would remain that way. Is that what you really want? I don't think so. When you look at it that way, I think you will agree you really do not want or expect it to *all be done at once*. Do not get anxious, guilty, or anything else negative when cleaning house. Take credit for what you complete.

If you are perfect,
only the perfect will be comfortable with you,
and
you'll wind up lonely....
Anonymous

Ready? Let's begin…again

Chances are, you have taken a break, but now you are ready to start again. *Good for you.* You are learning to GO WITH THE FLOW that leads to your goal. That is the greatest of accomplishments.

Because these next areas are a big challenge, the gratification you get when you finish will be more than you can imagine.

Cleaning the open areas of attics and basements may follow either the rule for cleaning the house, or the rules for cleaning the storage areas. Read through the rules for storage rooms or sheds to see which applies to the areas you have left to clean in the basement or attic. The rules you follow will depend if the items in these areas are more like the house, filled with furniture and antiques, or if these areas have a lot of storage boxes and trunks.

Storage rooms or sheds

If your storage areas are small, compared to a garage or basement, ideally you will empty the unit so you will have room to work. I do not suggest totally emptying the unit, then sorting and replacing the items. I suggest that you grab the first box or item and deal with it as needed. Place it in the appropriate cardboard box or pile neatly in various piles for organization. Separate into categories such as: baby items, children's items, toys, keepsakes, etc. Sort any box you remove and LABEL THE BOXES. Write short descriptions on at least one end of the box and on one side. (Otherwise, you can bet the writing will be the part of the box that is facing away from you when you are searching for something.) Labeling the boxes allows you to know at a glance later, what box you need to open. Have soapy water and cleaning supplies handy to clean the items you plan to keep.

This procedure allows you the ability to quickly re-stack the clean, organized items back in the storage unit. In the event of darkness, fatigue or interruption from rain (if the unit is outside). This enables you to begin again the next day or later, by removing the sorted items and to continue cleaning. Possibly you will clean and clear an area that will allow you to begin stacking in permanent organized piles so you will not have to handle boxes over and over, if delayed or interrupted.

As you work your way through the storage boxes, you may decide that sorting boxes filled with small items, such as papers or small keepsakes may reduce your cleaning speed. If this is the case, stack these boxes in a "To Do Later" pile. You may decide to take these boxes in the house and sort them by the fireplace or television.

Try not to leave these boxes in the house overnight, even if you need more time to sort through the boxes. This is a good way to transport critters,

such as cockroaches and spiders in from the outside. If you are present, you might see them and destroy them before they can set up a homestead. If you bring boxes into the house and leave them unattended all night… hello new tenants.

While sorting storage areas, TRY to keep yourself in a "Throwing Away Junk mode" This may be difficult, because you are often sorting items from your past. We are all guilty of *keeping too much*. On the other hand, *do not be too hard on yourself* if you feel you are keeping too many things. I have often been sorry later if I *forced* myself to toss something that I really was hesitant about throwing away.

IMPORTANT…Do not decide if someone else's stuff is JUNK. Ask family members to sort their own treasures, or enroll them in helping you clean the storage area.

I am sure that my ex-husband of twenty years *will never forget* when I decided to clean his gun cabinet. I felt it was untidy of him to keep his old hunting licenses and unused tags. I threw them away. I found out later. Once he had hunted a certain number of years without filling his tags, he could turn in his unused tags and old licenses as proof and get a "special hunt tag." Regretfully, I threw them away the year he was to qualify.

That was MY LESSON, in keeping my hands off other people's stuff. Believe me. It was a BIG lesson too. Neither of us will ever forget it. That was part of my being a *cleaning, control freak*. No one has the right to mess with other people's belongings. Even a small child may have a very important rock or stick. Tossing that item may break a toddler's heart. Take a moment and have a quick discussion with family members on what is important to THEM.

REMEMBER THAT ONE PERSON'S JUNK IS ANOTHER PERSON'S TREASURE. (If this is the only thing you learn from this book, I will feel I have reached my goal by writing it.)

Once you have cleaned everything from the storage unit or area, clean the storage unit itself. Knock down the cobwebs and sweep the floor. If the floor is cement, I suggest that you clean the floor, using a garden hose, to help settle the dust. Be sure the floor is dry before putting the boxes back in the unit. In any storage area, it is wise if you can put pallets on the floor first. (Or, you could use boards on bricks on which you will place your boxes.) This raises all your belongings off the floor in case water enters the area.

The belongings of a friend of mine were ruined when rain entered under the rented storage unit door. Her insurance policy covered the damage. However, no amount of insurance money can replace some items. How can you place a price on your childhood keepsakes?

If you stack your boxes several boxes deep, try to decide which boxes you may need to access most often and place those boxes at the front of the piles. I often put up small cardboard signs to tell me what is in the boxes, such as: kids' items, Christmas decorations, etc. Sometimes I will draw a diagram of the unit, listing the location and basic contents of the boxes and tape it to the door of the storage area. You think when you are cleaning, that you will remember where the boxes are later, but believe me when I tell you that you will not.

The box contents list can be as detailed as you wish. Some will simply list the boxes by the titles you have written on the outside of the box. Others of you will make special notes, such as...Parts for baby crib in box labeled "Kids Items", or Aunt Grace's vase in the box labeled "Never Throw Away." This makes it easy to find the ugly wedding gift Aunt Grace gave you, so you can display it on the fireplace mantel when she decides to pay you a visit.

My list may look something like this:

WHERE IS IT?
- BABY ITEMS: Back right corner, back row.
- CHRISTMAS DECORATIONS: Left side, near the front, second row back- (behind Halloween box)
- GAMES KIDS WILL GROW INTO: Behind "Kids Toys" on the back wall.
- ETC.

My daughter-in-law Michelle tells me that with her system, she marks the top edges of storage boxes with different colors to code her boxes.
- PINK: Baby items
- RED: Christmas items
- ETC.

Garage
How you clean the garage, will depend on the condition of the disarray. If there is plenty of room for you to work, you can use the *"select a wall method",* or even select part of a wall and follow the procedure with which you are familiar.

If you have absolutely no room in which to work, you will need to pull items out, as you did in cleaning the storage unit, clean the items, and then sort and label boxes as you go. Pile these boxes outside the area you are cleaning, until you have cleared a space large enough to work. Be sure to stack boxes with the labeled side out for easier organization.

Once you have cleared an area, you must decide if you will clean the ceiling, walls and floor and if you will paint. Follow the procedures for the decision you make. If you are working in an area piled with items and boxes, you may wish to delay painting until you have more room, after you sort, box, or throw away. Hopefully, you will fill *many* boxes for donation or the garbage.

Once the freshly cleaned or painted area is dry, begin stacking boxes in categories. Continue following this procedure, as you work your way through each portion of the garage. Eventually, you will end up standing in the center of the room surrounded by labeled cardboard boxes stacked against the walls. Place signs above or near the boxes to identify their contents.

Once you have all the boxes stacked, you will need to clean the open center area. You may also decide to paint.

Pegboard, shelves and containers

Using pegboards, shelves and containers is the way to go when organizing tools and miscellaneous items. Small items such as nails, screws, hooks, washers and small repair items will store fantastically in small plastic containers. Many people will buy storage drawers, but small jars such as baby food jars, work great too. You can even nail or glue the jar lid to a wall or under a shelf to hang the jars with their contents in full view.

Pegs are great for tools and items when dumped in a box become a snarl of junk. Hanging hand tools on pegs will clear up the workbench or shelves for other items, eliminating a big search when you need a screwdriver or pair of pliers.

Shelves are necessary in storage areas and garages. They get items off the floor and utilize wall space that otherwise would go unused. You can never have too many shelves in these areas.

Other garage items

The garage will house many strange and questionable items. If you are a woman and there is a man in your home, I strongly suggest that you enroll him in cleaning the garage when it comes to dealing with items that you are not familiar with. However, if you decide that *you need to clean* these areas, please be aware that there are NEW RULES for cleaning here.

Understand that unless you are knowledgeable with these items, it is impossible to place them in proper order. Something that looks like it may go with a carburetor may belong to something totally different. You may think that the garage is in such disarray that the man of the house is unable to find anything. This may even be close to the truth. Believe me, it will definitely be the truth, if you clean this area without knowing what you are doing. (You do not want to suffer the wrath when something breaks on your car and he is able to only find one of two parts, because you separated them while cleaning.) If you feel you must go ahead with this project. Here are some suggestions.

Clean and organize what you can. Make piles for all items ranging from small, medium and large. If they are in boxes, leave them in the boxes, but stack them in piles. Get the male members of the house to commit to at least fifteen minutes a day or every other day, to go through the stacks and piles to organize them. If they come across items to which they need easy access, one of you can place them in a spot that you have cleaned on the workbench, pegboard or shelves.

You may be surprised how easily your husband or son willingly sorts and organizes the garage items. They may work only the time they committed to, or they will jump in and get it done. Remember, by now, the men in your home have seen what you have done to the house. They may have fear for their prized possessions and will organize them to protect them. On the other hand, they may have little or no interest in your cleaning project. If this happens, I suggest that you dust, box and organize as much as you can without totally dismantling the place. Label boxes the best way you can and pile them neatly out of the way.

As big as a job as this was, do you see how you could sort a couple of boxes a day and clean a couple of articles a day until you finish the job? You do not have to kill yourself to get this job finished.

Make it a goal to always work at a pace that does not cause havoc in your life.

CHAPTER 20 <u>THE YARD</u>

The Yard

Your housekeeping is unseen by the general public. Your yard is more like a badge worn on your sleeve. Even the stranger from out of town can drive past and see your yard. As members of the community, I feel that we do not have the right to inflict the general public and our neighbors, with our decision to keep a messy yard. Our yard is part of our neighbor's world and we owe respect to our fellow neighbors. No one has the right to dictate to anyone else how to keep their yards, but I feel we owe it to each other to keep our yards presentable.

I do not believe there is a person around who really cares if a yard needs mowing. It is upsetting, however, to view a collection of old cars, batteries, piles of tires and debris. There will always be that perfectionist neighbor who wants you to take care of your crab grass, so it does not bloom, go to seed, and infect their yard. It is up to the individual homeowner to have crab grass or not. Crab grass may be disrespectful in someone's eyes, but junk is disrespect in everyone's eyes.

Even the best of yard keepers can tolerate what they may consider junk, if it is kept in an orderly fashion. In the suburbs and in small towns, yards often display a variety of items. Stored boats, campers, and woodpiles stacked against the storage shed are commonplace. These are usually in the back yard.

Front yards for the most part are usually storage free, displaying a fence, a walk bordered with plants and flowers, and often bushes and flowers around the house and fence line. In Arizona, the yards are often the natural desert.

Each person will decide what kind of yard he or she will have and how much care the lawns will need. If you love to dig, water and putter in the yard you will have all the ingredients for that hobby. Your yard will more than likely become a showplace that even the stranger would enjoy.

I am not the gardening type and now I am at that point in my life where I want to sit in a manicured yard without doing yard duty. This gives me several choices. Hire someone to do my yard work, or keep it so simple that it requires only minimal effort on my part to keep it nice.

Most people will care for their own yards, but if you can afford one, hire a gardener. You do not have to hire a professional gardener. Teens are always looking for after-school jobs. You can have the yard of your choice without lifting a finger.

Unlike Arizona, not having grass is seldom a choice in an area where it is natural to have grass. A decision to avoid grass in states like Oregon or

Washington is virtually unheard of. In these states, barren ground is shabby and distasteful. However, even in a green state, you can reduce your grassy areas to small patches surrounded with river rock or wood chips for easier care. Once you have installed the river rock and wood chip areas correctly, they need very little attention.

To begin

Start in one corner of the front yard. Rake and clear one section at a time. Clear the yard of all-useless items, junk or debris. Continue this procedure following the fence line around your property. Then go around the perimeter of your house. Once you have cleaned these two perimeters, you have only the center area of the yard to finish.

This method of cleaning your yard can be spread out over several days or several weeks. Like the house and garage, you can clean the yard in spurts and at your own pace.

Once you have the yard cleaned you will make decisions about plants, flowers and the landscaping of your choice. As tacky as it sounds, artificial flowers are one option.

I will never forget when a neighbor in Oregon asked me to water her grass while she was away. Faithfully every day, I watered her lawn, taking special care to sprinkle her beautiful pansies so they would survive her absence. Upon her return, I boasted that, even with my "purple thumb" her pansies survived. I continued to tell her that I made sure that I watered them every single day. Laughing, she thanked me for my attention but added that the pansies were artificial. I am sure that as you read this, you are convinced that is why I have a "purple thumb" if I am unable to tell an artificial flower from a real one. However, for weeks after that, I would ask everyone who visited what he or she thought of Judy's pansy patch? Every single person thought that they were beautiful and real.

I have a neighbor in Arizona that has pots of artificial flowers sitting in her front yard and they look great. To avoid looking at the empty pot that sits by my front door, I am seriously considering artificial flowers myself. At least I would only plant them once. Actually, I guess I could buy several types of flowers and interchange them. Right now, I keep planting new ones when the others die. If you do use artificial flowers and live in a state where you have definite seasons, please remember to take the flowers in during the winter. (Unless you do not care if you have flowers sticking up through the snow.) If you leave the flowers out through the winter, the secret is out about the artificial flowers.

If you chose to have real plants and flowers, select plants that require the attention that you are willing to give them. Landscape your yard so that it requires as little care as possible. This is good advice, even for the person who likes gardening. The gardening enthusiast would rather spend their time fussing with a new type of plant or a new item in the yard, than unnecessary weeding or trimming.

Grass

When you own any grass, you must be responsible for cutting it. If mowing is not your thing, hire one of the neighbor kids to do it for you. Unless you really enjoy cutting grass, I do not think anyone has the right to steal the job of the local teen that cuts lawns for extra money.

By keeping your yard simple or edged with wood chips, it becomes an easy procedure to zip around the yard with a lawnmower. For the person that finds mowing the lawn a chore, it is very annoying to have to mow around freestanding items, plants and patches of flowers. This is why; if you have lawn ornaments, placing them in your flowerbeds will remove the hassle of mowing around them.

Lawn ornaments

Lawn ornaments can be fun. They range from cutouts of chubby women and men bent over in the flowers, to humming-bird feeders or elegant statues. Ornaments display the taste of the owner and what they like to view as they enjoy their yard. It is a great way to have fun in the yard. I personally had a colorful birdhouse that I enjoyed, but my favorite was a multi-leveled planter, tiered like a wedding cake, in which I grew fresh strawberries. I loved being able to pick the live, fresh fruit. However, I was careful to keep some distance between the birdhouse and the strawberries.

CHAPTER 21 <u>PETS</u>

Pets

Pets are lovable creatures that require care, love and freedom to be them selves. Like children, pets also need discipline. If you do not discipline your pets, they become animal brats and people will not like them. Loving your pet does not mean that everyone else will fall in love with him or her. They need to be lovable for others to be attracted to them. What you think is "cute" behavior may not look so cute to a guest. No one wants to dislike our children or pets, but no one enjoys a child or pet that is rude, disrespectful or being a nuisance. We must do all we can to help our children and our pets develop into family members that others will enjoy being around.

I believe that pets deserve certain rights in the home, but they also need boundaries. Boundaries teach the pet how to live in harmony with all the family members, human and otherwise.

Human family members do not deserve having their possessions chewed or soiled and they have the right to sit on furniture that is pet hair free. Everyone should feel comfort in preparing a sandwich on a countertop without wondering if a pet has walked there recently after exiting a litter box.

Just as children have their rooms, a pet needs a place of his own. It may be a basket in which to sleep or a blanket in a designated area where he can go and get away from the toddler who is pulling his hair. A mother cat may want a cardboard box in a secluded corner of the basement when she is ready to give birth.

Although a pet will need a place of his own, it is usually not a good idea to let a pet claim a piece of furniture for himself. Even if you keep the furniture covered with a blanket and remove the blanket when guests arrive, the pet may spend the entire evening wallowing the guest who sits in his chair. If nothing else, he may sit and stare at the guest with an evil eye all night.

Pets get lonely when left for long periods of time. During this time, they may become destructive. I am not sure if it has been proven that they destroy things to get even or because they become bored and are trying to find something to do. Do not have pets if you are not going to be there for them.

Always protect your pet with a fenced, protected area to play out-of-doors. Educate yourself by reading books on pet care and by securing training for your family pets, so they can be among the best of the family members.

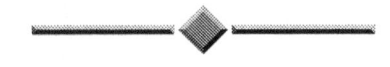

SPRING AND FALL CLEANING

Did you ever wonder how the-tradition of spring and fall cleaning began?

In the "olden days", as many would call it, there was no central heating or air-conditioners. Wood and coal were the main fuels for cooking and heating the home. These types of fuel often smoked up the house, leaving soot and a smoky residue on the interior of the house.

In the spring, when it was time to open the windows and doors for ventilation, people thoroughly cleaned their homes to get rid of the smoke and soot.

Homeowners then endured an unending battle of dust all spring and summer, as the dust filtered through the open doors and windows. In the fall, it was time to close up the homes for winter and began using the heat. Eager to end the dust battle and to prepare for the long winter of being housebound in a clean home, people thoroughly cleaned the home again.

This is why the tradition of spring-cleaning and fall cleaning was initiated.

CHAPTER 22 SUGGESTIONS AND CLEANING

Answering machine
TIP: Unable to see the settings on your answering machine because the raised letters are the same color as the machine? Use whiteout or nail polish to paint the letters to make them easier to read.

Bathroom
Use shelves and pegs in the bathroom, to hold hair dryers, make-up, hair products and towels. It is a great way to have items handy and clears the countertop for a neater look.

TIP: Electrical plugs are usually marked with a rough texture to indicate that it is the top of the plug. It is very difficult to see. In fact, I never knew it was there for years. It is better if you mark the top of your appliance plug-ins with fingernail polish or whiteout to designate what is the top of the plug so you will put the plug-ins into the electrical outlet correctly on the first try.

Books
Books are valuable possessions and they belong on bookshelves. Unless books are all lined up neatly, by size, for example, a set of encyclopedias, I personally do not like them in the living room. I prefer enclosed bookshelves. I think open bookshelves look the best in the bedroom, study, or office. However, if anyone is allergic to mold, you will want to keep from storing books in the sleeping area of the allergic person. Books have mold and dust in their pages and it gets worse as they age. Select where you place your books according to your likes and needs.

Boxes (cleaning)
After you have cleaned each wall and each room, you placed all excess items into boxes that designate what you wish to do with them. You must make yourself deal with the contents of these boxes before continuing your cleaning. Double check the boxes that you plan to keep to see if you can place more items in the Donate or Give-Away boxes.

Busy work
Do busy work while you watch television. You will be surprised how much you will be able to do. You may find that you are so absorbed in what you are watching that you are actually unaware of what you are doing. Imagine your surprise when you look down and see that stacks of folded laundry surround you. In addition, you have completed the hand mending plus opened and sorted the mail. During the commercials, you scanned your

magazines and tore out the articles you wanted and have a sack of magazines for the recycle plant or to go to the garbage. Just remember before you go to bed put away all that you accomplished. Do not leave them until tomorrow. Pick up as you go.

Bypassing

When you do daily maintenance you may have to bypass things that need done. You will concentrate on what stands out and demands the most attention. You may choose to bypass most of a room to be able to allot time to a room or project that needs it more. However "bypassing" is a temporary action. Go back later and give the chore you passed its rightful allotted time. This could even mean that you fall behind, but this is OK. Just keep your goals in mind and you will get back to it. It is important that you learn to bypass without guilt and without conjuring up a "Black Cloud." The knowledge that it is a temporary action should keep the "sunshine" in your life.

Ceilings

To whiten acoustical ceilings use a bleach-water spray (one-third bleach to two-thirds water). Be sure that everything is removed or protected with plastic to prevent discoloration to furniture, fabrics and carpets.

Ceramic tile (Non-floor)

Ceramic tiles on walls or countertops are cleaned in the same way as floor tiles. Wash with soap and water. Use a toothbrush and cleansing powder for the grout or spray with bleach and water solution to whiten the grout. It may be necessary to use a grout cleaner then seal with grout sealer. For best instructions see your tile dealer.

Clean-up teams

Design clean-up teams for Saturday chores. Start with a great breakfast together as a family. Do something special. It can be anything from animal-shaped pancakes to a family member taking a turn each week selecting the breakfast menu. Have the teams set out to do their chores with the goal to be done as early as possible so family members can do what they wish for the remainder of the day. It can be a family event such as the zoo or a picnic or it can be everyone doing his or her own thing. Keep it an exciting and interesting day by mixing work with fun. Be careful to keep that occasional water fight during the watering of the yard or while washing the car to a few fun moments. Otherwise chores may fall to the wayside. This is a positive way to teach children about doing chores.

Coupons

Many people save and use coupons. If you are such a person the rules are simple. *Keep all coupons together.* It does not matter if you keep them in a drawer, file box, or a cardboard box. Just keep them in one place.

Decorations/Keepsakes

What to do with wall decorations or knick-knacks that hold a special meaning for you, but no longer fits into your decorating theme? These are usually things that were made for you by your children or grandchildren. Place them in the family room or study. Eventually they may end up in a trunk in the attic. Even your children expect them to end up in the attic but they do expect you to keep them.

Dishes

You can use paper plates to avoid washing dishes but you will still need to collect and dispose of them. The best control you can have of dishes is to *confine eating to the table.* Ideally each person, once they finish eating, would rinse their dishes and place them in the dishwasher or toss the paper plates in the garbage.

If you allow people to eat all over the house, it soon becomes cluttered with dirty dishes and spilled food. Add in some tossed clothing, newspapers and personal belongings and you will see how easily a house becomes cluttered and messy.

After dishes are placed in the sink or the dishwasher, the designated dishwashers only have to add soap and wash. Remember to take a few more minutes and put the clean dishes away. It is great to start a fresh day with clean dishes and an empty dishwasher.

Always wipe the stovetop and countertops after washing dishes. If you have another second or two quickly sweep the floor and take out the garbage. Time yourself to see how much time you actually spend on the kitchen after a meal. I think you will be surprised how little time it takes.

Dusting

Feather dusters will push the dust off the item you are dusting causing it to land somewhere else. Use a cloth dampened in water or furniture oil to pick up dust from hard surfaces. Use the vacuum for soft surfaces. When using furniture oil you must polish oiled surfaces with a dry paper towel or cloth to remove the oiled residue or the oily surface will attract dust quickly.

Fall cleaning

YOU DON'T NEED TO DO FALL CLEANING.

Fireplace

Fireplaces can be fun. However, they are messy to clean. If your fireplace has an exterior clean-out door you will simply sweep all ashes into the hole in the bottom of the fireplace and remove the ashes through the clean-out door. Do not put warm ashes into garbage or disposal can. Warm cinders can start a fire.

Fireplace flues need to be cleaned periodically to be sure that soot does not build up inside and catch fire. Cleaning flues is very messy and you need to be sure that it is done correctly. Hire a professional.

Sparks that pop out of a cozy fire can start fires. Always keep the fireplace screen in place or the glass doors closed during use.

If a fireplace is not in use, heat may be lost up the chimney if the flue is not closed. If you close the flue you must remember to open it when you start a fire later or you will fill up the house with smoke.

I had a chain with a hook on one end and a metal tag on the other. I taped the words FLUE CLOSED on the metal tag. Whenever the fire was out and someone closed the flue we put the hook through the round hole in the flue handle. This way the tag hung down into the fireplace. It was impossible to miss the tag when anyone put wood in the fireplace to start a new fire so they would remove the tag and open the flue. When not in use, the tag would rest on the hearth so it could be easily located when needed.

WARNING: If you close the flue THE FIRE MUST BE OUT. Cinders may appear to be extinguished but they can smolder for days. If you close the flue when there are still warm cinders in the fireplace, carbon monoxide will fill the house poisoning all the occupants. A good way to be sure the fire is out is to *remove all ashes from the fireplace before closing the flue.* This does not mean to simply push them down the clean-out hole. You must also remove the ashes from that area before closing the flue. **This warning is not to be taken lightly. Carbon monoxide is an odorless killer.**

Every owner of a fireplace should have carbon monoxide detectors placed throughout the home.

To remove soot from the face of your fireplace you can use a small portion of an acid mixed with soapy water and clean with a brush. Since it is a toxic acid, I am not giving you the name here. Go to your tile store to buy the product and to get the proper mixing instructions. You must follow the mixing and the handling of the acid carefully. While you are there ask if they can recommend safer product-to clean soot from the face of the fireplace. (Also see GROUT)

Floors

Vinyl and washable floors—These floors need mopping often. You are unable to have a clean house without mopping floors. The only way to make mopping easier is to use an electric scrubber. Even then you will use a mop to wipe up after scrubbing.

I do not suggest using a sponge mop for cleaning floors. Wiping up a spill without bending over is a great reason to use the sponge mop. It's a new millennium. *Exercise is in. Bend over. Wipe up that spill.* To me, using a sponge mop to clean a dirty floor is much like raking the yard with a toothbrush. I have never used a sponge mop and felt that I did any serious mopping. I am unable to figure how to get enough water on the floor with a sponge mop, then soak up the dirty water without working myself to death wringing out the mop. I was never able to clean corners successfully with a sponge mop.

Give me a string mop any day. I am able to get plenty of water on the floor and in the corners. It is really like "swabbing the deck." It wipes up quickly and easily, allowing me to grab some of the strings of the mop and wipe out the corners. If desired, there are plenty of buckets, bucket attachments and mops that allow you to wring the water out of the mop without getting your hands wet.

I reserve my sponge mop for scrubbing tall walls and ceilings. They are also good for washing high interior and exterior windows and any other hard to reach places that you wish to reach without a ladder.

If you have babies or toddlers in the home it is a good idea to run over the floor each day with a damp mop or wet broom of your choice. The dust looks better on the mop than on the baby.

Ceramic and tile floors—Floors of ceramic and tiles, such as Saltillo and Mexican tile, require special cleaning. It is best to clean and care for these floors by following the instructions suggested by the manufacturer or the store that sells these types of floors.

Carpet floors—Carpet will always require cleaning. You can hire a professional to clean your carpets, which is the easiest way and the most expensive. For a few dollars you can rent a steam cleaner and do-it-yourself. If you own or rent a cleaner, I suggest hiring a strong teenager to run either machine. It will save your back and give a teen an opportunity to earn some extra money. For this job I would pay my own teen.

Occasionally use a damp cloth or sponge and wipe up the dust around the edges of your carpet next to the wall where the vacuum misses.

Carpeted entryway—Nothing looks worse than entering a home on worn and faded carpet. One suggestion for an entryway where the carpet is badly worn is to replace the carpet with a vinyl or tile. Even the most amateur do-it-yourself person can do this.

Decide how much of the carpet you wish to remove and what shape you want the entry. You can cut it in a square, rectangle or make it circular. To mark for the rectangle or square, open the door and mark a couple of inches past the extended door to know how far to go out from the threshold. Make other marks several inches past the side of the door to indicate the cut lines there. Your goal is to have the door pass over only vinyl or tile when it swings open. If there are windows or glass blocks beside your door you may want to include them in the entryway.

If you wish to have a circular cutout you will need a string longer than the door is wide.

Tie a pencil to one end of the string. Have someone hold the opposite end of the string in the CENTER of the doorway. Make sure that the string allows the pencil to be several inches past the opened door.

Mark the carpet. Using the pencil, start at one wall to the side of the door. Swing it out and around to the wall on the other side of the door. (A pencil may not mark the carpet but it will give you the line to mark. You can use anything to mark the cutting line-straight pins, pushpins, chalk, etc.)

Once you have a half-circle drawn. Use sharp scissors or a carpet knife to cut out the carpet piece. DO NOT CUT THE CARPET ON THE LINE. Leave some extra carpet for the edging you chose.

Lay the tile or vinyl making sure that the edge slips under the cut carpet. (About four inches for vinyl.) Wrap the carpet around the tack strip and nail down or use a metal edging that you can nail or glue in place. Measure and measure again, if necessary, to be sure the door will always pass over the new flooring, not carpet. If you are unsure how to edge the entryway with tack strip or metal edging, your local do-it-yourself store will give you detailed instructions.

It is a good idea to remove the door threshold to lay new flooring. If you are laying ceramic tile it makes a nice finish if you lay the tile to the outside edge of the entrance and down to the first step. Replace the threshold with a shiny new one and you will have a very professional looking job. If you replace the threshold do not forget to get a new door sweep to match.

If laying vinyl in the entryway you can reuse the threshold if it is in good shape but you may need new screws.

If you are renting your home you may not be allowed to put in a new entryway. In that case you can cover a worn carpet with a throw rug. If the door will not pass over a throw rug you can use smoked vinyl runners.

Furniture
Get rid of furniture that cannot be cleaned or is broken. Donate reusable excess furniture to charity. I know that apartments are often small. Instead of jamming a lot of furniture into a small place, store it if you wish to keep it until you get into a larger home.

Wood furniture—Your goal may be to re-strain or repaint the furniture you now have. This can usually be done with a light sanding and a fresh coat of stain or paint using a spray can or brush.

If the furniture is badly worn, scratched or scarred it may be wise to strip the pieces to the bare wood before re-staining or painting. Stripping must be done in a well-ventilated area or out of-doors. Protect your porch, patio or garage floor with newspapers or plastic. When refinishing, never use spray finishes on windy days. If you ignore this warning you could end up paying for a new paint job for your neighbor's car or house.

If the wood finish is stain and appears only to be dirty, wash well with a good wood soap such as MURPHY SOAP. Rub with good furniture oil, such as OLD ENGLISH dark or lemon oil. Wash wood furniture at least once a year and rub thoroughly with oil. Maintain the wood by occasionally rubbing with an oiled cloth and buff to a shine. The rest of the time, use a good furniture polish.

If you decide to strip your wood furniture, an alternative to reapplying varnish is to rub the piece with linseed oil then rub with furniture oil.

Fabric furniture—Furniture comes in many fabrics. I like velour because I can clean the furniture over and over again and it cleans up like new. It can be cleaned easily with soapy water and a sponge and you can steam clean it with great results.

Other fabrics often require professional cleaning that does not last. I have known people who out of desperation to clean their furniture have removed the couch and chair cushion covers and laundered them in the washing machine. This resulted in clean cushions that clashed with arm and backrests that were dingy. Sometimes the cushion covers faded. Usually the covers shrank so the cushions no longer filled the couch.

If you decide to buy a couch but wish to find a nice used couch, consider going to an estate sale. These are great places to find good furniture. The furniture is often in very good shape and the prices are often very reasonable. However, I have seen estate sales with prices equal to those of a new couch. It will depend on your area and who runs the sale. Once you find an estate sale company what has good prices, give them your name and telephone number. Often, they will advise you of upcoming sale dates.

I seldom buy leather or vinyl furniture. I found them too hot in Arizona and too cold in Oregon. If you have pets or small children, I would stick with velour furniture.

Grout (to whiten)

To brighten white grout on the fireplace or in the bathroom, mix one-third bleach and two-thirds water in a spray bottle. Spray the grout with a fine mist. (Protect fabrics with plastic drop cloths.)

Housekeeper (hired)

Should you hire a housekeeper? If you can work it out to employ a housekeeper for even a few hours, I suggest that you look at that possibility closely. Money spent on cleaning frees you and your family so you can spend time together doing something more enjoyable. Most of the time it is worth it. If you do not feel that it is in your best interest to hire someone to clean, perhaps you can exchange favors with a friend. Possibly you can watch a friend's children for a few hours a week in exchange for her doing some cleaning. If there is a will, you will find a way.

How about hiring a teen for a couple of hours after school one or more times a week. Teens like to work around the supper hour. They have after-school projects then they study in the evening. A set time for a job each day or each week works well for a teen. If you prefer, he or she can watch the baby or kids so you can delve into cleaning that bedroom or basement.

Ironing

My favorite ironing story was when I was a new mother. I did not want to work outside the home, because I wanted to stay home with my two babies. In my search to earn some extra money I put a flyer on the bulletin board at the local coin-laundry that I would do ironing in my home. Most of my customers were single men who needed white shirts ironed. However, one customer was a woman who worked at the bank. She would sprinkle her clothes, roll them up tightly and fill a laundry basket to the top. It was so heavy that she could barely carry the basket into my house. It was during the time that permanent press clothes were showing up on the market and most of her clothes were permanent press. When it was time to do the woman's ironing; I put her dampened clothes in the clothes dryer and hung them on hangers immediately upon removal from the dryer. If I even ironed her clothes at all, I would occasionally steam iron the collars, cuffs and belts, but only on some garments. I would quickly press a seam into each sleeve and pant leg so they appeared ironed. Doing her ironing took very little time and it was so easy.

The woman was always excited that she could pick up her ironed clothes the very next day. She was amazed how fast I ironed, especially since I had two babies. She was equally pleased with the nice job of ironing I did. She even told me that no one had ever ironed her clothes as nicely as I did. The dryer did most of the work and I accepted the compliments and the money. She paid me a very good price to do her family ironing. Don't be like this woman, use your head not your time or money.

Junk drawers

Select one junk drawer to clean or clean them all in one day. Check each item to see if it has a true home elsewhere, if it does move it there. Decide if the item has value enough to keep. Wipe out the drawer and do one of two things:

1. Arrange the contents in a manner that makes some sense to you.
2. Dump the remaining contents back into the drawer.

If you find a piece that is broken off of something or is part of an item, put it in the junk drawer. Mark it first with a piece of paper or tape identifying the item. Otherwise, you will not remember what it is later until you have thrown it away. (It may be a good idea, to jot on the note where you found the piece you add to the drawer, if you are unsure what it is.)

Junk or Keep files

When I read magazines I will tear out articles that I want to read later, date them, staple the pages together and put them in my "To Read" pile. If I like the articles and want to keep them, I put them in the appropriate file in the file cabinet. My files include Health, Diet, Child-rearing, Car Repair, and Tax information. Then once a year, usually when I clean my files for income-tax preparation, I will go through all my other files. If any of the articles are still valuable I keep them. Dates on the articles will tell me if they are still applicable to the present time.

Keys

Are you and other family members always searching for keys? Put pegs for keys near the door or in some other designated place. You can also place keys in wooded or woven trays or baskets. Place the tray or basket in a common area and when everyone enters the house they drop their keys there. For men, the wallet valet or a tray or basket on his chest of drawers is ideal. It will hold his wallet and the contents of his pockets, such as coins, sunglasses, keys, etc. It is accessible only to people who enter his bedroom and it is handy when he changes clothes, showers or dresses.

Kids rooms

It is a good idea to have a lot of toy boxes and drawers in kids' rooms. Shelves are nice but not if you want organized shelves. There is no way a toddler will have organized shelves. It is easier on everyone if playthings can be dropped out of sight.

If there are too many toys in a child's room, he or she will have difficulty enjoying their playthings. Small children do not do well with making too many decisions. It is better that they have a few familiar toys with which to play. When a child becomes bored, introduce a stored toy to the room. At that time or a little later, remove a toy that the child shows less interest in. This toy is not gone forever; it may return at another date.

Toys that are not in the age group of your child should not be in his or her room. If they show no interest in the toy it is only junk to them. To keep a child interested in their toys, rotate the toys in cycles just as you would if they have too many toys.

Using the cycling method is a great way to handle children's clothing too. Keep only the clothes that fit your child now and the next few larger sizes. As your children out-grow their clothing, pack them up and bring out new sizes. If you decide to store unused children's clothing in the child's room DO NOT STORE IN PLASTIC BAGS. Plastic bags have no place near children of any age.

Plastic crates appear to be the perfect storage containers for children. However, if you place plastic crates in a child's room, you may want to fasten them to the wall or floor. Otherwise, children will soon discover that they can turn the containers over and stand or climb on them. You do not want to encourage your child to be jumping off of a crate in a room filled with toys or use it to climb onto suspended shelving. You definitely do not want to learn that your toddler used the container to climb up to a window, push-out the screen and tumble out a second-story window.

Additional storage drawers can be established under the bed. You can purchase the cardboard drawers that fit under the conventional bed or you can use a waterbed frame or a captain's bed. If you are even semi-good with tools you can make a bed pedestal containing drawers. Cut old dressers apart to use as a frame. Using a piece of plywood and boards for a box to hold the mattress, bolt them to the top of the dresser drawers.

Since small children's clothing is short you can also put chests-of-drawers in their closets.

I think it is always best to store outdoor toys outside on the porch, patio, or in the garage.

Warning: In kids' rooms, be sure that netting designed to hold toys is secured so a child will not become entangled, resulting in suffocation or strangulation. Put protective covers over electrical plug-ins to prevent electrocution. These covers are a good idea even if the child is older. You can teach a seven-year-old how to remove a cover if needed, then feel confident that when smaller children are visiting they do not have access to the plug-ins. Remember, if you have window blinds, be sure the pull strings are cut and separated. Do not leave the cord in a loop in which a child of any age can become entangled.

Kitchen

TIP: Never know which side of the lid to open for the sprinkle holes on the spice containers, pepper boxes, etc.? Mark those lids with fingernail polish or whiteout.

Knick-knacks

As you sort through your collection of items, you will probably find that you have a surplus of knick-knacks. Give them away, sell them, or pack them in a box and rotate them. The latter is a wise choice. You will be able to show all your prized possessions, just not all at the same time. It will add variety to your life. This does not mean that you will never buy another knick- knack, because you will.

When you do buy a new bobble to display, replace one you are already showing. Retire the replaced item to the rotation box. Be sure you mark your storage boxes clearly with FRAGILE. You may want to write an inventory sheet and attach it to the box so you can find your prized possessions at a glance.

The only time you will want to display multiple knick-knacks would be if you have a collection of figurines or something like salt and peppershakers. Ideally, you will want to display them under glass, in cabinets or on shelves. Do not set them out in the open unless you are willing to dust and wash them often.

Laundry

Laundry needs a designated home. You need a place for dirty clothes on their way to the laundry room or dry cleaner and you may need a place for dirty laundry once it reaches the laundry room. A place is also needed for clean clothes that need folding or ironing and for laundered clothes returning to the owner.

When we built our home I had my husband cut a hole in the bottom of the bathroom cabinet, providing a drop through chute to a cabinet in the bathroom below. Since the basement bathroom housed the washer and dryer, this was perfect. All dirty laundry ended up near the washing facilities. I could open the cabinet, wash what I wanted and the rest of the time the dirty laundry was out of sight. Since we built our home ourselves, I added the chute into the blueprints. I got the idea from a friend I had as a child. They had a square hole cut in the bottom of one of their closets, they dropped their dirty clothes into this hole, and the clothes landed in a pile in the center of the basement.

As good as this idea sounds, *it is a safety hazard*. After we moved into the house, my son was born. We had a stern rule about keeping the bathroom door closed at all times. A heavy-headed toddler would not survive a nosedive onto concrete. Even though my daughters were six and eight, I had to keep a keen eye on them and their friends so they would not be careless around the chute. In addition to occasionally climbing up or down the chute, they would often lean way down into the chute to talk to someone or to try to get the attention of someone in the basement. It was an easy way to communicate between the levels. If you wanted to speak to someone on the opposite floor, you opened the door to the clothes chute and yelled their name until they came to the chute to talk to you.

Clothes hampers are the best idea for collecting dirty clothes. When I say "hampers" I do not mean that they have to be purchased hampers, those are seldom inexpensive. Hampers can be wicker or woven baskets, with or without lids. There can be family hampers or hampers in the laundry room. There can be hampers in each bedroom and in the bathrooms. Laundry baskets work well if you wish each family member to have their own. A laundry basket in the bottom of each bedroom closet is ideal. (Even a cardboard box serves its purpose here.)

LAUNDRY RULE: If it is not in the "hamper" it will not be washed.

You may wish to have two hampers for each room. WHY? Most people are happy to have clean clothes but not grateful enough to put them away. Unless you will be policing each bedroom in the house, which I strongly suggest that you do not, clean clothes and dirty clothes will become mixed. I learned this when two of my nieces stayed with me during a family emergency. Instead of putting her clean clothes away, it was easier for Cathy to drop the stack of clothes down the laundry chute. It was probably more fun too.

I have found that people, who do not put away fresh laundered clothes, somehow manage to keep them separated from the dirty clothes, unless a roommate unaware of the process mixes them together. Select a light-colored basket for clean clothes and a dark one for dirty clothes or write CLEAN and DIRTY on cardboard boxes. (You could have the occupants decorate the boxes themselves, as a rainy day project.)

This means that the person doing the laundry, if other than the owner, will probably use the same dark basket to take the clothes back to the room. It would be a nice gesture to place the cleaned laundry into the other basket, rendering the "dirty clothes basket" EMPTY. If the person doing the laundry is not in the mood for nice gestures, it will be the owner's responsibility to make the basket switch. If the owner of the clothing is doing his or her own laundry, share this method with them.

If you find laundry baskets are too small, large woven baskets can be purchased at import stores. These can be a great way to get the laundry off the floor and furniture. NO GUARANTEE PROMISED.

Do laundry often. You can easily have enough dirty clothing to do laundry daily if your family has three or more members. Anytime enough clothes accumulate to make a load, wash them. Remember, for the best-looking laundry; separate your clothes before washing. Separate into piles of whites, light colors, darker colors, dark colors, rugs, rags and towels for cleaning the house and car. You also need to separate by type of wash, such as, gentle, permanent press, and delicate.

Do you know you can use your laundry softener sheets more than once? The first load never uses up softener sheets. On some solid-colored clothing, I have found marks from the laundry sheets if they are fresh. I will always use the "used softener sheets" on the solid-colored clothing that was previously stained.

If you put clothes on hangers when they exit the dryer they will require little ironing.

Dry Cleaned Clothes—It is a good idea to have a designated spot to put clothes for the Dry Cleaner. Remember if an article of clothing is not in that spot when the clothes go to the cleaner, *better luck next time.*

Leftovers

At least once a week, inventory the refrigerator and remove and toss all leftovers. If the thought of throwing away fungus-plagued leftovers haunts you, take a moment and toss that leftover the minute you hear your brain say, "I need to throw that away." Do not close the door telling yourself, "I will do it later." Remember to "Pick Up As You Go." Includes tossing molding food when you see it. It is the easiest maintenance of all.

Lists

Warning: Lists are not to be held heavy over your head.

Making lists is the best way to stay on top of what needs to be done and they will prevent the "Black Cloud" from following you everywhere. Trying to keep a list in you head will bog down your mind and exhaust you. Writing down things that you need to remember gets them out of your head and down on paper.

I am a master list maker. I make lists for everything. If I think I need something but cannot remember what it is, I can check my lists and remind myself immediately. I keep a list in the kitchen, the study, and sometimes there is one in the upstairs hall. Occasionally a list even appears in my bedroom.

You can put items you need to do and/or need to buy on your lists.

For example: One of my lists may look like this.

Buy printer ink   Get stamps
Milk   Bread

Call travel agent about vacation	Paint is chipped by the TV plug-in
Paint is chipped by the desk (outside wall)	Re-caulk bathtub
Buy 90-minute cassettes	Copy cassette for Anita
Owe both sisters a letter	Tell Maralyn I saw Paul
Buy pencil lead	Get battery to put in gold watch

This list is an anything-goes list. You can organize it into TO DO, TO BUY, TO FIX, TO CALL, etc.

If you have a family chalkboard, everyone can add to the list. Simply copy it on-to paper every couple of days and clear the chalkboard.

REMEMBER that you will NEVER complete everything on the list and that is not your goal. Your goal is to know all there is to know about your home and make decisions that make things work for you.

Other lists could be like the following,

TO DO

Spray fireplace with bleach spray

Dust over all doorways. (You thought of this one, when your son's tall friend was standing in the doorway and grabbed on-to the doorframe. When he took his hands down, they were all dirty.)

Wash light fixtures

Mend

Glue edge of desk where trim is coming loose

Clean linen closet

You can keep a notepad and pencil in every room of the house and keep a running list in each room of things that need to be done or need purchased. When you are ready to go to the store, collect lists from each room and make a master "TO DO" list

One thing about a shopping list… REMEMBER TO TAKE IT WITH YOU.

Decide how you will work from your list. You will be surprised how much you will accomplish in ten minutes a day. If you are able to donate a larger time slot to your list, do one of two things. Set the timer and work until time is up or draw a line across the page and stop when you get to that line. *Never make the entire list your goal.* Even though you know the list is on going you must find a way of indicating that you have completed tasks on the list.

Logbook

A blank book in which you write "Things You Want To Remember" is great for keeping records of all sorts of things. Record anything from when the furnace was last serviced to when you last had a physical. You can even write down the day that your spouse promised you that *one-day* he would take you on a luxury vacation.

Maintenance

Cleaning as you go means to do what needs to be done when you see it. When you are sitting on the toilet and you see something that needs to be done, do not ignore it. When you see that dust bunny behind the bathroom door or the muddy water dripped by the towel rack, grab a rag or paper towel from under the sink and wipe up the offending creature or design. How long does it take? Ten seconds? Before you toss that wet paper towel or put back the wet rag take a quick inventory. See anything else? Take a moment to wipe off the back of the toilet or the rim of the toilet. It only takes a few seconds more of your time.

This, by no way means that you will to do major cleaning when you see one little thing that needs attention. "Maintenance cleaning should take place everyday."

Magazines

If you are a collector of magazines and feel that you cannot throw them away because they contain something that you wish to read later, rotate your magazines. Decide the number of magazines you feel you want to have within your reach at all times. (I suggest twelve magazines.) Get a magazine rack if you do not have one now and place the chosen twelve in the rack. Understand that you can have a magazine rack in every room but the stack must never exceed approximately twelve.

Place all extra magazines in a cardboard box in storage or in the garage. Mark the box MAGAZINES and add the date. You do not have to file magazines by month or year or anything like that. The *storage date* gives you an idea of the contents.

When you notice that the magazine rack is filling up you will simply remove nine to twelve magazines from the top of the stack and place them on the floor. Remove the remaining magazines and take them to storage. Put the newest magazines back into the rack until it fills up again. Once a year or every other year when you clean the storage area you will decide if you want to dispose of a box or two of magazines. This way if you ever need old magazines you will know exactly where they are.

When you are running through the house "Picking Up As You Go" with octopus arms, you will forever-collect magazines and place them in racks. Magazines belong in the racks unless they are being read.

Make up the bed every day

It takes thirty seconds. Time yourself. If you make your bed as fast as you can, you can strip it, put on new sheets, a blanket, bedspread and pillow slips in two minutes flat. There is no reason that you cannot remake a bed in thirty to sixty seconds. It is your decision if the hemline is even with the floor, if the spread covers the pillows or if there are any wrinkles. We don't care. You will feel better about your bedroom if you make the bed in some sort of fashion.

A good rule: Last one out of the bed makes it. If you share a bed, this rule could be one advantage to having your feet hit the floor first when the alarm rings.

When to change the bedding? —You will establish this rule. If you sleep alone and bathe before bedtime you probably will not wash your linen as often as someone else might. If you are a person who works a late construction shift and sometimes falls into bed exhausted with plans of showering in the morning, you will change linen more often. Be aware dust mites collect in linen. I once read that one-eighth of the weight of a feather pillow that is five years old is made up of live and dead dust mites and their feces.

One woman I interviewed did not put sheets on her bed. Her reason, *then she didn't have to launder them.* She slept on the mattress cover and a bare pillow.

Mending

Avoid storing clothing in a box or basket and calling it mending. If you aren't going to mend, call it what it is-storage.

Mending is a great way to get the longest wear out of clothing. Replace a button, sew a ripped seam and put in a hem that is coming loose. All of these things will add to the life of your clothing. It does not take very long to make these repairs but a lot of us procrastinate when it comes to mending.

I liked the old days when Mom would sit in front of the old radio listening to the stories of the hour and mending socks. No one mends socks these days. We toss them and buy new ones. However, any hand mending you do have can be accomplished in front of the television at night.

Hems, buttons, and even most mending can now be done on sewing machines. I procrastinate, because it is a struggle to set up the machine, drag out the mending, and then do it. However once I am started I usually do quite well.

I volunteer at a nursing home in Tucson. I do mending for one hundred nursing residents. Yet, I will seldom do my own mending. One day, I decided that each time I did mending for the nursing home I would mend at least two items for myself. I figured I would get closer to having the mending done than I am now. If nothing else, perhaps I could keep the pile from growing.

I find it unbelievable that I would volunteer for the very job I have the biggest problem with. Possibly I know sub-consciously that volunteering a good way to get myself to mend.

Mirrors

There is nothing like a well-placed mirror to add a new dimension to a room. A sparkling clean mirror is beautiful. Do-it-yourself stores sell mirrors of all prices and all shapes. A mirror placed at both ends of a hallway will give the allusion that the hall goes on forever. Tall narrow mirrors placed correctly makes the viewer feel that he is gazing into an adjoining room.

You can go for months without cleaning mirrors as long as no one touches them. Fingerprints and cooking grease, which are attracted to mirrors, usually clean up with ample supply of window cleaner. If cleaning mirrors does not appeal to you, please do not install them. Nothing in a house looks worse than a mirror with little or no reflection.

I suggest that if you do decide to hang mirrors that are without frames, buy the plastic holders that screw into the wall. There are several kinds. One kind will snap open so you can easily remove the mirrors. I prefer these because the screws holding the plastic supports are out of sight behind the mirror. I strongly suggest that you do not use adhesive or tape strips to mount mirrors. The chance of breaking the mirror later during removal is high.

Nursery—SAFETY IS FIRST

It is natural to want all baby products handy for caring for an infant. Please be sure that these products are out of the reach of a child standing in the crib. It does not matter if he is not standing yet. There has to be a first time for everything.

This also applies to the sides of the crib. If you wait until the baby stands in his crib the first time before you lower the mattress it may be too late. The baby who is capable of standing is also capable of falling out of the crib because the sides are too low. A good rule is to lower the mattress when crawling begins because pulling up is the next step.

Diaper pails in the nursery are never a good idea. Most parents use disposable diapers but often keep the diaper pail to soak clothing soiled with baby food and other soil. If you decide to use a diaper pail and to put water in it, *do not keep it in the nursery*. Remember that toddlers are head-heavy and if they fall into anything head first they seldom can get out on their own.

Anyone can drown in a teaspoon of water. This is why you need toilet locks on the toilet lids in your home when you have toddlers.

Octopus

Definition: An eight-armed, human cleaning machine. All arms work continuously as the being passes through the home.

Painting

Before you begin painting check with your painting store for the latest tips. They offer a wide variety of products from drip pans that attach to the roller when you paint ceilings to rollers that open-so that you can pour paint into the rollers. There are always new and different ways of doing things. Before beginning any new paint project ask the paint store clerk what's new.

Paint touchups

When you see a place that needs paint touchup, place a sticky note on the wall at eye level stating where to paint or draw an arrow in the direction of the damaged paint. Remove the note once you put the location of the "spot" on one of your lists. If you fail to do this you can walk around with paint and brush for hours dabbing at walls. Days later you will find a place you wanted to paint most of all. You will wonder how you could have forgotten it.

Papers to keep

Legally, they say you should keep papers that pertain to taxes or legal transactions for seven to ten years. I usually keep most receipts that long. I have felt a little silly when I am looking through boxes of papers that are labeled with seven to ten-year-old dates. I find old telephone bills, old electric bills and a purchase slips for the refrigerator or radio. I tell myself that I really do not need to keep all this junk, and then comes a letter in the mail that proves me wrong. For example:

"You qualify to join a class-action suit against a company that held your mortgage during the years 1986-1996. If you can forward all payment information from that time you will be included in the class action and share in any settlement." Hey, don't laugh. I received a check for seventy-five cents once. Another time I sent in copies of my phone charges for a certain year and got twenty dollars of free long-distance calling that the company owed me from overcharges.

On a different occasion I received a five-dollar credit from the phone company because I was able to send proof that I was a client during a specific time. Perhaps one day the reward may be higher.

I remember one particular time when keeping receipts really paid. When I purchased a waterbed I was promised a *lifetime supply* of waterbed treatment for my bed. I could always stop by the store and pick up my supply of solution. After about five years the store said that I had to show my receipt to get the water treatment. It seems that everyone was just stopping by and claiming they bought a bed there. Handing out free water treatment was getting too costly for the store. I was one of the very few who had the original purchase receipt. Later a new company purchased the store. They said that they did not have to adhere to the old policy, so I could no longer get the solution for my bed. I used that bed for almost fifteen years before replacing it and I have only purchased the treatment solution for the last two years.

Phone calls

When you receive phone calls you do not always have to sit down and chat. Sometimes it is an invited break. However, if the call lasts over ten minutes, get moving. Pick up things. Dust the furniture. Do some exercises. Just do something. If you are in a big cleaning mode, time your calls, so you will get back to work. Do not let phone calls feed your procrastination. A telephone with a headset is perfect for chatting and allowing you both hands to clean.

Plants (dusty)

If weather does not allow you to take your houseplants outside for a sprinkling, use the shower as a communal bath. They love it. Leave them until the excess water has drained and return them to their homes.

Quiet Time

One necessary rule I believe that every parent needs to establish is a rule that parents need time alone. Often there are things that need to be discussed and not in front of children. My husband and I used our bedroom as our "Quiet Place." We would announce that we had something to discuss and the children were not to knock on the door unless it was very important. When the children were small, we began with individual short sessions until they learned that we were always accessible if they really needed us. Be prepared if you use the bedroom for your quiet place. Once your children reach their teens, you will receive comments and knowing looks when you leave the bedroom. "How was your TALK?" They will ask, followed by plenty of giggles and rolling eyes.

When an individual parent needs time alone, it is called "Mommy's Quiet Time" or "Daddy's Quiet Time." This is usually done when both parents are home or someone else is there to care for the children. The children learn that they are not to knock on the door unless disaster has befallen the ON DUTY adult. Since the kids know that you are normally accessible, they are pretty good about giving you your time. You may need this time to finish a report for work or to work on your hobby. You may just need to lock yourself in a room because you feel as if you will go over the edge if one more rubber sneaker slides down your shin.

Recipes

Everyone has hundreds of recipes. There are many of different ways to file and organize recipes. Toss them in a drawer, type on index cards or store in a computer. Whatever method you chose to file your recipes, just be sure that they are in one spot.

Round-Robin Cleaning

Definition: A method of working on a chore or task in small time segments without pressure. It is having the ability to accomplish a job at your own pace, such as washing one window a day. This allows you to reach a goal without the "Black Cloud" covering your "Sunlight."

Screens

Clean window screens with a soft brush and plenty of soapy water. You can stand the screens to clean or lay them on a flat surface. Rinse with a garden hose or under the shower.

Shopping

If you are able to do any of your shopping during the evening mealtime or late at night, you will make the process faster. These are the times when people are normally at home with their families so the stores are less crowded.

Always be careful if you go shopping late at night. Always park your car as close to the store entrance as possible. Keep alert and watch your surroundings as you approach your car. Look under the car and in the backseat before getting in. Have your groceries in a basket, not in your arms. Be ready to make quick get-a-way if necessary.

ALWAYS REMEMBER, no one is capable of taking you anywhere if you are "dead weight" lying on the ground. Drop your car keys, grab your chest, roll your eyes back and drop to the ground. If a criminal is going to take the time to stab and shoot someone who just had a heart attack or fainted, they were going to kill you anyway.

If you have a small child with you, be sure to land on the child, so the child is not easily accessible to the criminal. Hopefully, the startled crook will run or grab your keys and drive off in your car. No car or any amount of money is worth dying for.

Spring-cleaning

FORGET SPRING-CLEANING.

Stairs

If you have a second floor, you may want to try what I have found works for me. Designate a visible spot at the top and at the bottom of the stairs, where I put items that belong on a different floor.

Instead of running up and down the stairs with single items, I pick up everything that is waiting for a ride to a different floor. My pile at the bottom of the stairs always contains some paperwork because my office and files are upstairs. So on one trip I may have papers, a pair of earrings, a sweater, a pair of shoes and a new bottle of bathroom cleaner. When I reach the top of the stairs I put the cleaner under the bathroom sink, the shoes in my closet and the earrings in my jewelry box. I hang my sweater and place my paperwork on my desk. (I will file them later.)

As I head down the stairs, I will pick up the items at the top of the stairs. An invitation to stop by the Ford dealer to try a key they sent me to see if I won a car. (I accidentally carried it up with some paperwork.) There is a different sweater to go downstairs; it has a stain that I need to remove before it goes through the wash. There is also a grocery bag in which I had dumped the contents of the wastebaskets from my office and the upstairs bathroom.

Once downstairs, I will put my invitation by the phone so I will not forget to go. (I just know that one of these days I will win a new car.) I lay my sweater on the kitchen counter while I grab the kitchen garbage and head outside to the can taking all the trash I have collected along the way. When I return I will treat the spot on my sweater and put it in the laundry room for tomorrow or put it in the designated spot to go back to my personal laundry basket.

Television remotes

TIP: To avoid unending searches for the remotes, make designated places to keep them. My father always had a small shelf beside his chair that held his remotes. You can also make pockets out of fabric to hold the remotes and drape them over one arm of a couch or chair. Another idea is to place Velcro on the wall near the couch and Velcro the remotes to the wall.

Time It

Anytime a job seems like a big job or you find yourself procrastinating, time it. Often you will discover that it takes less time than you thought it would. By timing jobs it may give you more incentive next time the job appears. It will also help you in your time-management. It makes it easier on your busy schedule for you to "sandwich in" a chore.

Toilet

A quick cleanup that works quite well is to drop denture cleaner tablets in the bowl when it is filled with water. You know the kind, they fizz and boil and remove food and smoking stains from dentures. Start with six tablets and check for results. Do again if necessary. If the denture tablets do not seem to have an effect on the stains, you need to go to the "get tough" method mentioned in chapter 13, The Bathroom.

Wall decorations

Most people find that they have surplus wall decorations. Use a rotation method of storing these in clearly marked boxes and then rotate them on the walls. Just make it a rule to always take something down when you put up something new. If you don't you will continue adding until you reach a *cluttered look*, the very thing you are trying to avoid.

I am sure that you have visited someone or been in a store that was overcrowded. It was all very nice but there was just too much of it. When you left you may have had to take a big breath of air to escape the claustrophobia you were feeling. Personally, after I visit someone who has too much stuff for my comfort, I go home and start removing things from my walls. Honest, I might go several weeks before I put anything on the walls. It is as if I need the space to handle the overcrowded feeling I encountered.

Window coverings

Drapes and curtains—Drapes and curtains are nice window coverings but often require dry cleaning. *Unless you are willing to clean them once a year or every other year* do not burden yourself with curtains or drapes.

Vertical blinds—Vertical blinds are decorative and require little care. (Dry cleaning may be required if you choose fabric vertical blinds.) If you have sliding glass doors, you may find that verticals are necessary here. If you have an emergency and need to you can exit the house right through vertical blinds. Vinyl blinds are exceptionally good if you have small children or pets. You can use a wet sponge to wipe away handprints and smudges.

Mini-blinds—Mini-blinds do require some cleaning but they are easier to care for than curtains or drapes. The metal minis will damage easily. The paint can chip or fade and the slats are easily bent and cannot be straightened again. If you have small children or pets, it only takes one curious peek out the window and the blinds will bend. Wood minis are very nice but more expensive.

Vinyl minis are easy to clean and look very much like the metal blinds. They are inexpensive to replace if damaged. Often you can cut the vinyl minis yourself to fit your window. As a rule you can cut one and-three-fourths inch to two inches from the sides of the vinyl blinds before you reach the mechanism.

When shopping for vinyl minis, check where the mechanism is placed in the header of the blind. You can cut within three-eights inch from the mechanism. Using your window measurement, check the blind at the store to see if you can cut enough off the blind to custom fit it to your window if necessary.

To customize your vinyl minis you will need a saw. It is also helpful to have a miter box to help you get a straight cut but it is not necessary. The mounting brackets will cover the cuts you make. You will also need a good pair of scissors.

You have a choice of mounting the blind inside the windowsill, or mounting it outside the windowsill on the wall. Mounting outside the sill will not require cutting the blind at all. Simply center and mount, following the enclosed instructions. However, if mounting inside the windowsill you will need exact measurements.

When measuring for the inside mount, be aware that the blind has mounting brackets for the header. These brackets are fastened to your window frame to hold the header of the blind. Be sure that your final cutting line allows for those brackets. You may want to mount the brackets, and then take your measurement for the blind header.

The brackets are designed to attach to the header of the window or the sides of the windowsill. Select which is easier for you. Sometimes the header is constructed of steel making it difficult to drill holes.

After cutting the blind header, check the cut by slipping the header into the brackets. If you are trimming the maximum amount from the blind you may not be able to fit the header into the brackets until you cut some of the slats. However, you should be able to see if the fit is correct. You will have room for error because the brackets are about an inch deep. You want the header to fit as tight as possible inside the brackets. If you cut the header too short it will move around in the brackets when you raise and lower the blind and it could slip out. With the header in place or while holding the blind in position on the window, mark where you want the last slat. The last slat will ideally hang a fraction of an inch above the bottom windowsill or it may rest lightly on the sill.

Lay the blind outstretched on the floor. The bottom bar on the blind houses the end of the cords that operate the blind. Use a kitchen knife to pry out all the plugs from the bottom of the bar. Lay the plugs aside. The goal here is to get the cords loose from the bottom bar. Do not bother with trying to untie them. Simply cut the cords off. ONCE THE CORDS ARE LOOSE FROM THE BOTTOM BAR...DO NOT PULL THE ADJUSTMENT

CORD THAT RAISES AND LOWERS THE BLIND. If you do you will unthread the blind. You don't want to re-thread the blind.

Starting at the bottom, gently remove one slate at time until you reach the slat that you have marked to be the last one. (Keep the slats you remove in case you need to repair your blind at a later date.)

To cut the slats you will use a different measurement than you used for the header. You may remove a slightly different amount from each side of the blind because the mechanism is closer to one end than the other and you wanted to cut off the maximum allowed. (This measurement difference goes unnoticed.)

Measure from the hole where the right cord drops out of the header to the edge of the right windowsill. Deduct one-fourth to one-half inch. Mark that measurement on the first slat of the right side of the blind, measuring from the hole through which the cord passes to the end of the slat.

Repeat the measurement for the left side and mark the left side of the first slat. Cutting the blind slightly narrower than the header allows your blind to hang freely without binding up when opening and closing. If your window frame is constructed of stone or bricks that vary in size, you will need to find the narrowest point for your measurement so the blind will function freely.

After you have marked all the slats that need cutting, use the end of one of the slats you removed from the blind to mark the correct curve you want on your cut line. If you do a nice job of cutting the first slat, use the piece you removed as a pattern to mark all the other slats by drawing around it. By doing this, all slats will be uniform and no one can tell that the blinds have been customized. Using scissors cut the slats you have marked for cutting. (If you cut a slat incorrectly, you have extra slats to replace the one you cut in error.)

Once all the slats have been cut, hang the blind in the brackets. Remember—DO NOT PULL THE ADJUSTING CORD, IT IS NOT FASTENED TO THE BOTTOM BAR AND WILL PULL OUT OF THE BLIND. Check to see that you have enough slats to reach the bottom sill. Be aware that *the bottom bar will be the last slat.* You need to cut that bar now.

Use one of the cut slats to mark this bar. Be sure to line up the holes in the slat to the holes in the bar, for the correct cut. (Allow for the end caps when marking for cutting.) Remove the end caps to cut with a saw. Replace the caps on the bar, thread the pull cords through all slats and through the bottom bar and tie in a big knot. Trim the ends of the fabric "ladder" that support the slats about six inches longer than the blind. Wad up these "ladders" and stick them into the hole on the bottom of the bottom bar and replace the plugs. NOW YOU CAN PULL THE CORDS TO ADJUST THE BLIND.

With the blind DOWN, cut the draw cords to the desired length, cut the loop and knot each string or attach pulls. **If you leave a loop, children or pets can become entangled and strangle**. You must be sure that the blinds are fully extended before you cut the cord. If you cut the cord with the blind in the "up" position, you will not allow enough cord to close the blind.

If you have large windows that seem to require custom-made minis, be aware that you can hang several blinds in one window. My favorites are the big windows with smaller windows on each side that open. Install three mini-blinds on these windows. (Each blind will fit each part of the window.) This is very nice when you want to open one small eighteen-inch window for ventilation and do not have to open eight-foot of blinds, forfeiting your privacy.

If your vinyl minis come with a header slat, you can decorate it with wallpaper or fabric to match your color scheme. Wallpaper paste will work well on the header slat. For fabric, sew a tube and gather on the slat. This allows you to customize each blind in each room. You can also add draperies, flounces, or curtains over your minis.

Cleaning minis is fairly easy, especially vinyl. You can dust them with a wet sponge or cloth but at least once a year, I like to clean them thoroughly. Remove the blinds and put them to soak in the bathtub filled with warm, soapy water. Do not let the metal or wood minis soak. The paint will flake off of both types of blinds and the wood will get water logged. Using a soft scrub brush and sponge, wash the blind thoroughly. Rinse in the shower and stand it on end in the corner to drip. Remove excess water with a towel.

I personally like to use a large flat place to clean minis, such as a deck or driveway. With the blinds fully extended, I scrub them with warm, soapy water and rinse with a garden hose. Then I can stand them to drip or hang over a clothesline. I like to lay them on a piece of plastic to dry with a towel. If I wash them inside, I sometimes lay them on a sheet for final drying. Of course, you can always hang you minis damp and dry them in the window but you have a good chance of getting water on your freshly cleaned window. When I am in a hurry, having a few drops on the window to wipe off is nothing.

Cleaning minis may sound time-consuming, but you will be surprised how fast you can run one through the shower and re-hang on a clean window. Keep the "round-robin" method in mind. How many days would it take to wash all the mini-blinds in the house if you wash one mini-blind a day? Do not get hyper if you discover it may take ten to fifteen days because we are talking fifteen minutes out of each day.

Wiping up

Wiping up becomes your mission. You are like an octopus walking through the house with each of your eight arms wiping, picking up, and straightening. You become a cleaning machine on feet but guess what? At first you are conscious of each movement, after a while it will come as naturally as chewing gum and walking. It will come so easily that you will not even be aware that you are doing it.

Right now, you may walk upstairs to use the bathroom and that's all. With practice, on the way up you will find yourself-carrying up a pair of shoes, a jacket and a package of toilet paper. When you come down you will bring down a folded dishtowel that accidentally was put in with the bathroom towels and a picture you wish to put in a letter to your mom.

The same thing goes for walking through any room. When you exit the room you have items in your hands and when you re-enter the room you have items in your hands. Do not step over a shoe or book to get a soda from the kitchen. Pick it up. Drop it in the correct spot or the "drop off area at the stairs."

If you wash the dishes
and make the bed every day.
When visitors come,
they will see that you did do something
that day.
Pauline Zigler (my mother)

CHAPTER 23 <u>MAINTENANCE</u>

Let's walk you through an example of a MAINTENANCE DAY. Remember this is just an outline. I myself may not do everything in one day that I write here. I may do more, do less or change the routine. This is a guideline, a way to get you to acting like an automatic cleaning machine so you will do it every day without thinking about it. You will choose what maintenance schedule works the best for you.

The alarm rings. You jump, get, or drag yourself out of bed. You stand and stretch. Turn immediately and straighten the covers on the side of the bed you exited. Walk to the other side and straighten that side. Walk back to the first side of the bed for the final straightening. If there is someone in the bed, skip this part. The bed-making job belongs to the last person getting up. If there are any shoes or clothes lying around, pick them up and put them where they need to be. Go to the bathroom. (If you don't have an automatic coffeepot, plug in the coffee first.)

Step into the shower. Lather up. Shampoo. Rinse. Replace all articles to their original resting spots, on a shelf or the corner of the tub.

Not today, but on a day in the near future, you will spray the shower curtain with a tub and tile cleaner or a de-solvent cleaner before you take your shower. Before you rinse yourself you will use the plastic-net body scrubber and give the shower curtain a quick cleaning. (Use your foot to hold the curtain taunt against the tub for easy scrubbing.)

Today, as you are rinsing, quickly rub the soapy net scrubber over the tile, tub edges, and tub bottom. Rinse the scrubber and hang to dry. Once you have dried yourself, before you step out of the tub, quickly wipe over the tile and faucets with a washcloth or towel to remove water beads. The use of a daily shower spray cleaner is an additional help in the battle of soap scum and water build-up. Wrap a towel around your head and leave the shower.

Once you are finished in the bathroom, take a quick assessment of the room. Are towels hanging on the towel bar? Is the rug neatly draped over the edge of the tub? Have you tossed your make-up in the make-up basket or put shaving items away? Did you put away your toothbrush and toothpaste? If the mirror was steamy did you use that moment to quickly wipe the mirror? The room should look the same or better than when you entered. If you can get everyone in the house to pick up after them selves in the bathroom, it will greatly reduce the cleaning required for this room.

Coffee is ready. Fix breakfast. If you use a fry pan, rinse it while it is hot or use a paper towel to wipe it and put away. Return food to the refrigerator and quickly wipe off the stove and counters. Sit down to eat. Try to eat together as a family. Make it enjoyable. Let it be a quiet moment together before the new day begins.

Everyone will rinse their dishes under the water and place them in the dishwasher or sink on their way out of the kitchen. If you had one or more lunches to make, make them now if you did not make them earlier or the night before. If there are multiple people in the house, hopefully you will have some help. When you dressed, if you ironed something to wear, you either left the ironing board standing, in it's usual place or you put it away after use. You may take time to relax and read the paper or catch the news on TV before you leave for the office, drive a carpool for the kids, etc. You may or may not return home until the evening.

If your job takes you out of the house during the day, the first minutes after you arrive back home is the time that belongs to the children. Your life will be easier if you make that a rule. They will learn that this is when you are most available to them. You may chose this period to spend time with all the children at once with a group discussion. Later you can give individual time to each child.

Toddlers have missed seeing you all day but even a toddler will wait a moment until you are ready for them. They will be patient long enough for you to put on a pair of shorts or jeans or put away perishable groceries. Toddlers love having you at their level on the floor. Prepare to be sat on and wallowed. They need to talk to you and to get hugs. Grade school children learn quickly that once the babies get the attention they need, they will toddle off to find their toy friends, leaving behind a mother who looks a little disheveled but is willing to give them their time.

With older children, you can often catch up with the day's news while preparing dinner or cleaning the kitchen together. Make it a grand time to be together and you both will look forward to this time of the day. Just keep in mind that all the children need a time when they can talk to their parents in private. If you do not pick up on this need, it is to be hoped that your children know that they only have to ask and you can make yourself available.

After dinner and the dishes are washed wipe the countertops and sweep the floor. Now your evening begins. Following dinner is a good time for everyone to chip in and complete all the family chores that remain. If you do this daily, a few minutes of housework will be exactly that...a few minutes.

If you have schedules drawn up, most of the family will do their chores while dinner is being prepared and the kitchen cleared. Always utilize KID POWER whenever possible.

All that now remains is unfinished homework. Remember to give a child a break if they have a lot of homework, allowing them to join the family for a short time before continuing their studies.

Always try to have family interaction besides television—in the evening. It is a good rule to limit the watching of television. In our home, as long as it was daylight and weather permitting, children needed to be outdoors. After all, in Oregon there were many months when they were confined to the house because of bad weather. Record any desirable after-school television shows for the kids and let them watch them in the evening. Always encourage play that offers exercise and learning.

All children require routines at bedtime. Babies and toddlers need cuddling and quiet time before they sleep. A child is never too young to have a book read to them. Children are never too young to pretend to read to their parents. When the parent makes up the beginning of a story for a small child, the child will eagerly finish the story. This encourages the use of their imagination.

Pre-school children and young school-age children need a few quiet moments to read to you and to add anything that they forgot to tell you earlier about their day. These are good times for children to ask questions or share something special with you that may be bothering them.

Older children and teens need to have you peek in on them. They enjoy that you take a moment to knock on their door and ask how things are going or offer them some brain food to eat while they study. You may find yourself sitting on their bed sharing something from your day with them, opening up for conversation from them. Never think that because you are running late and you find the older sibling already in bed or asleep that you should pass them by. Tiptoe in and when they respond sleepily to your presence, apologize that you did not get by sooner and promise you will make it up to them tomorrow. Then make sure you keep your word.

The older child understands about time and the lack of time and they are forgiving as long as you keep your promise the next day. Always kiss the sleeping child, brush their brow and tuck in their covers. Even the slightest tucking gives a child of any age a secure feeling. Besides, it gives you time to view your growing child as you used to when they were smaller, looking like a sleeping angel.

If you have not completed the allotted cleaning time for the day, finish after the younger children have gone to bed.

Those last few minutes of the day are reserved for spending time with your spouse. It may be used to discuss the children, share the day's events or to pay bills. Always try to give yourself some time too, if only a few moments. Possibly you can invite your spouse to share a tub or shower and accomplish two things or more at once. Add some lighted candles for a wonderful quiet moment together.

If you do not have children your schedule may be more flexible but always keep it a goal of spending special time with your spouse. I think that often couples feel that since they do not have children to care for and feel like they have a lot of time on their hands, they will often overload themselves. By filling up their schedules with too many things to do, they do not find time for each other.

I have found that people, who do not have schedules because they feel that they have all the time in the world, often end up accomplishing very little. It is the largest of the procrastination traps. Be sure that you always have a routine. It may be a routine that varies or can be eliminated altogether if desired but have one anyway.

HOUSEWORK-DAILY

Always try to designate five to ten minutes a day to each room for maintenance housework. This does not mean to neglect hanging your bath towels until then or failing to pick up your dirty clothes when you made your bed. You may actually find that ten minutes is too much time. Yes that is what I said. Remember the bathroom this morning? You left it as clean as you found it. Does this mean that now you are supposed to get naked and clean that shower curtain? No, it does not. I will give you a lot of options and you can select a few.

Bedroom

Utilize the designated five to ten minutes. Set a timer if necessary to either keep you in there for the time allotted or to alert you when it is time for you to leave that room for the next one. Check to see that all clothes and shoes are put away. Perhaps you will sort through your gym-bag to be sure it contains clean clothing. You can run the vacuum over the floor and dust the furniture lightly. If you vacuumed yesterday, today you will just dust the furniture and straighten the shoes in the bottom of the closet. You might straighten a drawer or two or sit down and untangle several necklaces that have been on your dresser for several days.

How about attacking that cobweb you saw in the corner the other morning when you woke? Where did that mysterious little black handprint on the bedroom wall or door come from? Since you have a wet rag in hand, you may as well wipe out the windowsills and wipe the wall around the light switch. Today might be the day that you take your summer shorts out of the drawer under your waterbed and exchange them with the stack of winter sweaters from the closet. This could be the day that you "bypass" the bedroom by only lightly dusting because you have or had such a full day today. If so, make an honest promise to yourself that you will spend some extra time on this room tomorrow. *Then keep your promise.*

Bathroom

Everything looks good here. Wait! Remember yesterday while sitting on the toilet you saw toothpaste smeared on the wall at the end of the cabinet. You meant to wipe it off but Tommy fell and hurt himself and you forgot it. While you have a wet rag in hand, wipe the top of all the baseboards. (Count them…4 boards.) Since several days have passed without using window cleaner on the mirror, do that today. You may put something in the medicine cabinet that someone left out and take a moment to dust the contents, wipe the shelves and straighten them. Perhaps one of the children got a favorite towel and jammed the rest back into the cupboard. Fold and straighten the towels. In the bathroom you can never wash the walls or floor too much. Empty the garbage. (Was five minutes enough for this room? Was ten minutes too much time for this room?)

Hall

Run the vacuum. Dust a picture frame with a damp cloth or clean the glass on a picture with glass cleaner. Dust one or all of the baseboards. Always walk down the hall with a soapy rag in hand and attack handprints and scuff marks. If you continually attack marks on the walls you will never run into a major mess, as you would if you NEVER touched a rag to a wall then one day tried to wipe a mark. That is when it will make such a difference that the newly cleaned area brightly stands out as a clean spot on a dirty wall. The only way to overcome that dilemma is to wash the entire wall, then the ceiling looks bad so you wash it, then the hall no longer matches the other rooms, etc. You are just so much better off by doing routine "round-robin" wiping of hall walls on a daily basis.

Kitchen

This room needs little suggestion from me on how to fill your five to ten minutes. If you begin with a sink of soapy water and a rag, you will always find something to wash. The floor, the counters, cupboards, walls and woodwork are always eager for attention. Also waiting are the drawers, appliances, dishes, and spices. You can straighten shelves, cut vegetables, organize the refrigerator, empty the dishwasher and the list goes on forever. If you steal minutes from another room, you can always use those minutes here. Empty the garbage. (The kitchen's allotted clean-up time can be utilized following a meal if you do not want to return to this room later. I know I never do.)

Living room and family room

Walk through picking up anything that does not belong in this room. Then dust and vacuum. I usually make this my priority room because it is the room that welcomes visitors. I will find that I usually chose to spend more time cleaning this room. I will do the usual cleaning suggestions and then I will add an extra chore or two to my list. I may dust knick-knacks, polish furniture, clean windows, wash walls, clean the floor and anything else that I feel needs doing to put the room in its best presentable order.

What have you accomplished?

You have just completed the maintenance cleaning of five rooms, which took about five to ten minutes a room. That is a total of twenty-five to fifty minutes. Do you think that anyone can find that much time to clean house each and every day? I bet you will agree that every one of us can find even more time than that to clean, by simply giving up one or two half-hour television shows. Most of us can find time by cutting back on some of those phone calls that go on and on without really saying anything important.

The minimum maintenance cleaning will never work if you and the other members of the home do not routinely pick up after themselves.

Different ways you can walk through the family room on the way to the kitchen.

Pick up three-year old Tommy's' shoes and socks. Grab Jan's school backpack and the empty glass that you drank a soft drink from when you watched a few minutes of television. Set the glass in the kitchen sink, drop Tommy's socks in the laundry basket in his room and put his shoes in his closet. Put Jan's backpack in her room, dropping it on the floor inside the door. Remind her that she needs to get to her homework if she has any to do.

OR:

Walk through the house and request that Tommy and Jan meet you in the living room. When they arrive, ask them to please look around and pick up and put away anything that belongs to them. Remind Tommy to put his socks in his dirty clothesbasket and to put his shoes in his closet. Compliment him on what a big boy he is, then proudly tell him that you are sure that tomorrow he will remember to put them away by himself. When Jan grabs her backpack and gives you a dirty look, smile sweetly and remind her about her homework.

OR:

You can stand in the living room and scream… "You kids get in here right now and pick up this junk!" I do not advise this because it sets the tone for arguing, not to mention that they probably will act as if they did not even hear you. You may find yourself saying things like, "Jan, is that your backpack?" Which means. "Jan, pick up your backpack." DON'T do this. Say what you mean. "Jan, I should not be required to remind you about your backpack every day. It is your responsibility to put it in your room, not drop it on the way to your room. THANK YOU."

You may help to train them by giving them gentle reminders, such as "Jan, your backpack." "Tommy your shoes." By letting them see what is out of place or pointing out what needs to be done you will be training them to become a cleaning octopus. (Hopefully)

Now as a final exercise I want you to pick a day when you feel that the house is a real mess. You may choose to do this exercise before you even begin to clean using this book. You did read through the whole book before you began cleaning, didn't you?

EXERCISE

You are sitting in the middle of a messy house. Read the following instructions and follow them to the minute Time needed: 15 MINUTES.

Close your eyes. Breathe deeply. Clear your mind. Visualize that you are sitting in the living room watching television, dreading to get up and clean house. The phone rings. You answer, "Hello." The voice responds, "Hello, this is Joel Adams. I am a Secret Agent for the President of the United States of America. The President is very impressed with the suggestion you jotted on a postcard to him about his views on the Welfare Program. In the President's effort to connect with Real America, he would like to stop by for a moment and thank you for your support. I am sorry that we were unable to let you know that he was coming until the last moment. Security reasons you know. Oh, and by the way, Mr. President would like to have a drink of water and use the bathroom while he is there. We are in a motorcade in your city and will be arriving at your home in exactly 15 minutes. Good-bye."

WHAT DO YOU DO????????? Feel the panic?
Jump from your chair. Look at the clock. Get busy. You have only 15
minutes.

NOW THE EXERCISE IF OVER... How does your house look now? Different? I bet it does. Were you surprised at how much you did in such a short time? I bet the cleaning went something like this: Grab stuff out of the living room. Put it anywhere, in closets, behind the couch, in drawers, in other rooms, or even under the couch cushions.

Run through the center of the room with the vacuum. Continue down the hall with the vacuum to the bathroom. Grab the toilet brush. Quickly scrub the toilet. Yank the shower curtain shut. Take all the dirty towels, clothes and anything else in the bathroom that does not belong there and toss them in any bedroom and slam the door shut. Slam shut all doors in the house.

Put up new towels. Wash the bathroom sink, countertops and mirror. With rag in hand, drop to the floor gathering any obvious dust bunnies. Straighten the rug, spray the potpourri spray and run for the furniture polish.

Back to the living room, spray furniture tops with polish and briskly rub to a shine. Race to the kitchen and get a pitcher of water and ice. Place pitcher and eight glasses on a tray and place on the coffee table. (You do not know how many agents there will be with the President.)

Eyeball the situation. My word, you can see the end of the kitchen counter from the living room. Race to the counter; shove everything to the other end of the counter so it is out of sight. Grab the basket of fruit and place it on the counter that is in view.

Run to the bedroom; throw on a clean blouse, or shirt. Run to the bathroom. Wash your face and don't use the fresh towels. Dab on some lipstick, or after-shave lotion, and comb your hair. The doorbell rings. Your 15 minutes are up. "HE'S HERE."

This is an exaggeration. This is by no means the correct way to clean a house. However, I think it will prove how much you can get done in a short time-IF YOU HAVE TO.

Another good example of speedy cleaning is always demonstrated when staying at a motel. The motel room is very tidy when you drag in the suitcases. Let me paint a picture of the room while you are there.

The pillows are promptly pulled from under the bedspreads to prop viewers for watching television. The suitcases are opened. Some clothing is stacked on the shelf in the closet. Some clothes are hung. The shoes are tossed on the floor and some things are put in the dresser drawers. Toiletries are set on the vanity and the dressers. The ice bucket is filled. Possibly the plastic garbage can is filled with ice and warm cans of soda from the car.

The newspaper is read and scattered around the room, by one or several readers. The room is cluttered with snack containers and bags. Swimsuits and wet towels are hanging on doorknobs and on the shower rod in the bathroom. The floor may be scattered with toys. It begins to feel a lot like home. Because you are on vacation, it may be more relaxed than home.

How long does it take for motel dwellers to vacate the premises the next morning? Time it someday. Once you are all packed and ready to leave the motel, take one last look. I bet this is what you see.

There are unmade beds, towels on the bathroom floor and wastebaskets full. This demonstration shows that even if you messed the room up thoroughly, it can be easily and quickly cleaned because there is a limited amount of furniture and items in a motel or hotel room. What you can do in a motel you can do at home. Keeping your home simple and organized will make it easier to straighten up.

You Made it!

CHAPTER 24 COMPULSIVE BEHAVIOR

During the interviews I did for this book I heard many stories about housecleaning and the lack of cleaning. Stories ranged from having to remove shoes when entering the house to children locked out of the house in an effort to keep the house clean. There were stories of diapers piled in the bathroom until the husband wondered how many more the room could hold. Other stories were about homes that barely had a path from one room to another. I heard of large bags of garbage piling up on the back porch instead of being taken to the garbage can.

In contrast, some stories were about stark, sterile homes where families really never lived their lives. Homes that were plagued with rules, which were aimed at always portraying the look of a model home, instead of home filled with interacting families.

The "Black Cloud" of housework is in many of our lives because we put it there. Just as we put it there, we can remove it. Most of the time our cloud is something from within ourselves, which we may not even know exists. Once we are aware of our cloud we can work on escaping its shadow and letting light into our homes and lives.

Sometimes our behavior may be more than a cloud. It may be called "compulsive behavior." Everyone does something that borders on compulsion but once noticed they usually stop doing it. For example: I count the copies as they are being made on a paper copier. I set the counter for twenty-five copies and as it begins copying, I will silently begin...1...2...3. When I realize that I am counting, I will stop. However, if I am daydreaming, I can get the count pretty high before I am even aware that I am doing it. Why would I count the copies when the machine is counting them for me?

One person I interviewed said that she finds herself counting the groceries as she unpacks them. She knows it is stupid because there is no reason to count groceries. She doesn't count anything else. She said she does stop herself, only to find herself counting again. Another woman said that she would count her laundry as she folded it. Others counted stairs or cracks in the sidewalks.

One man told me that when he is at a stoplight, if he doesn't sing along with the radio, he finds himself counting how many seconds it takes for the light to change. When he first found himself counting he decided that it was a good idea. If he figured out how long the light took he would know when it was his time to go before it actually changed. Of course, this would mean that he would always have to count at every light to know when it was about ready to change.

Once this gentleman discovered that the lights were set differently at each intersection, he no longer counted. However, if he is not careful, he finds that he will slip back in to his counting habit without realizing that he is even doing it. He doesn't even know why he started counting in the first place.

Most people with compulsive-type behavior suspect that their behavior is not healthy. However, if they are unable to stop, they often keep their concerns to themselves. Just as often, people around those who appear compulsive do not talk about their actions and simply go along with them.

A husband may not initiate a conversation with his wife because he is aware that she counts everything, including the words in the newspaper. Interrupting her makes her upset because she will have to begin counting all over again. Many times a spouse will go along with their mate's obsessive cleaning by accepting that it's just the way that person is. If you make yourself live by strict rules that imprison you, chances are you are suffering from **O**bsessive **C**ompulsive **S**yndrome. If you are unsure if you are compulsive or wonder if you are in denial, asking others close to you may help. A family member or a friend can often point out behavior that they see as compulsive. If you feel that you do have a compulsive behavior problem please know that there is help available. Call a counselor or doctor today.

This brings us to the end of the book. I hope that you learned something new or different about housekeeping that will help make your life and the lives of those around you, easier and happier. My wish is that you destroy any "Black Cloud" you find and that SUNLIGHT will replace those clouds.

GOOD-LUCK

THE END

ABOUT THE AUTHOR

During her twenties and thirties, Laurel Zigler owned her own "Black Cloud" of housekeeping. She lived and raised three children in eastern Oregon. During those years, she claims her role was "Super Mom." Maintaining the perfectly clean house was the driving force of her life.

After years of trying, she finally escaped her "cloud." It took years of trial and error to be free of her perfectionism housecleaning that shadowed every corner of her life. She claims that the struggle to remain free is never ending. Like bad weather, you never know when a cloud might try to block the sunlight.

Curiosity encouraged Laurel to talk to others about how and why they keep house the way they do. She began interviewing and talking to anyone and everyone who would talk to her. During these interviews and conversations, she designed a simple exercise that often opened the person's understanding about themselves.

Laurel put all the information she learned from her own experiences and of those she interviewed into a book that she feels will help others escape their own "Black Cloud."

In 1979 she left the Oregon winters for the cactus and sun of Arizona. With her children grown, she now lives in Tucson where she loves hiking in the desert and the mountains. Laurel loves travel, and when she is not visiting her children and grandchildren, she is off to visit places around the world.

Laurel Zigler's first book, *WHEN I WAS A KID*, was published in 1996. This collection of autobiographical stories details the childhoods of those interviewed. All proceeds from the sale of this limited-edition book went to the Pio Decimo Center, a non-profit Community Center located in Tucson, Arizona.

The Author has plenty to say about *Escaping the Black Cloud of Housekeeping* and why she wrote it. She sums it up with one statement –

"If one person reading my book, finds the freedom and the peace that I did, it was worth the time it took to write it."